DREAMERS AND DESIGNERS

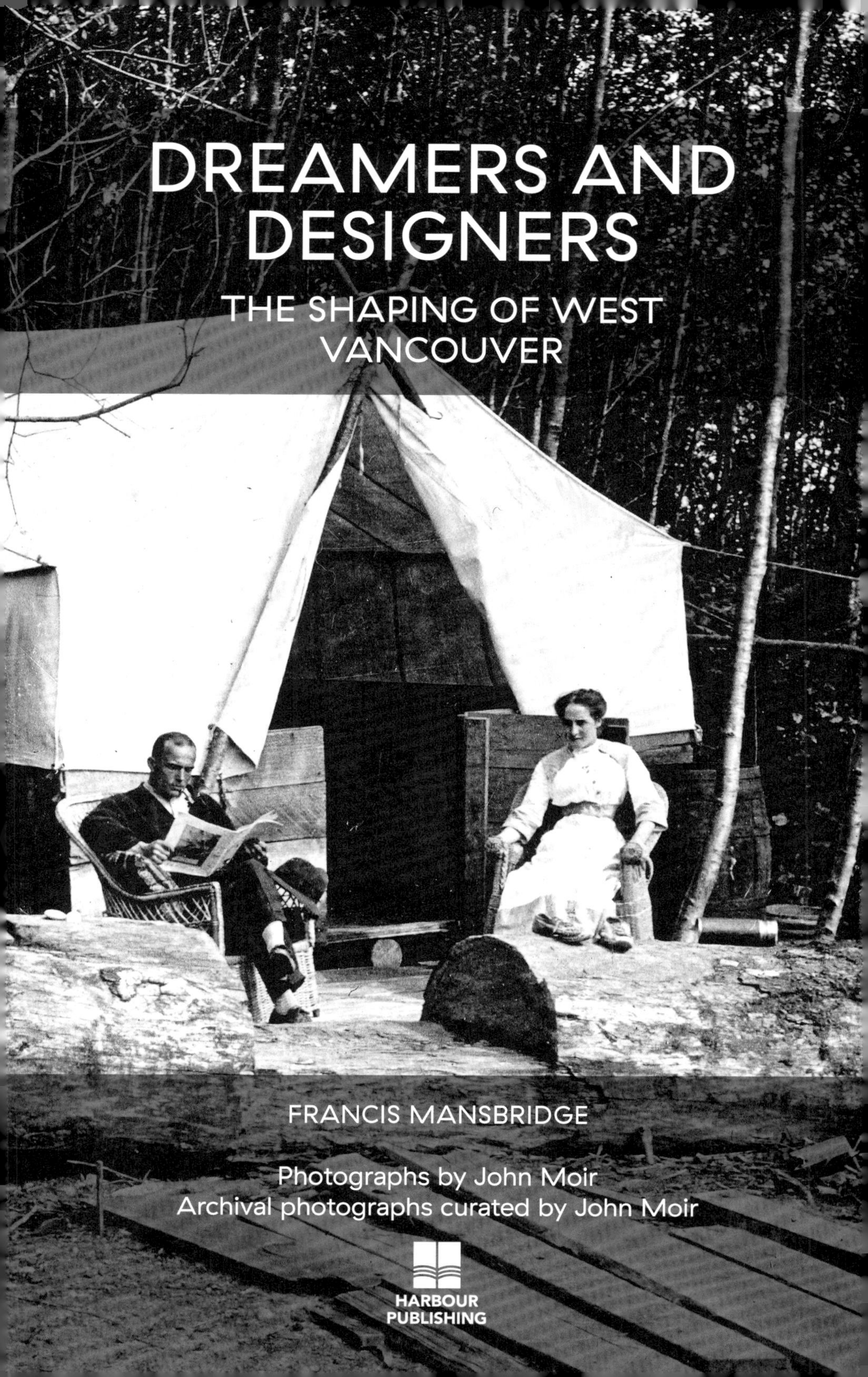

DREAMERS AND DESIGNERS

THE SHAPING OF WEST VANCOUVER

FRANCIS MANSBRIDGE

Photographs by John Moir
Archival photographs curated by John Moir

HARBOUR PUBLISHING

1 2 3 4 5 — 22 21 20 19 18

Harbour Publishing Co. Ltd.
P.O. Box 219, Madeira Park, BC, V0N 2H0
www.harbourpublishing.com

Thanks to the West Vancouver Historical Society for its strong support and contributions to the project.

Edited by Lynne Melcombe
Jacket design by Anna Comfort O'Keeffe
Text design by Roger Handling
Printed and bound in Canada

Canada Council for the Arts Conseil des Arts du Canada
British Columbia Arts Council An agency of the Province of British Columbia
Canada

Harbour Publishing acknowledges the support of the Canada Council for the Arts, which last year invested $153 million to bring the arts to Canadians throughout the country. We also gratefully acknowledge financial support from the Government of Canada and from the Province of British Columbia through the BC Arts Council and the Book Publishing Tax Credit.

Library and Archives Canada Cataloguing in Publication

Mansbridge, Francis, 1943-, author
Dreamers and designers : the shaping of West Vancouver / Francis Mansbridge ; photographs by John Moir ; archival photographs curated by John Moir.

Includes bibliographical references and index.
Issued in print and electronic formats.
ISBN 978-1-55017-851-7 (hardcover).—ISBN 978-1-55017-852-4 (HTML)

1. West Vancouver (B.C.)—History. I. Title.

FC3849.W48M36 2018 971.1'33 C2018-904923-5
C2018-905484-0

Dreamers and Designers: The Shaping of West Vancouver
is dedicated to the memory of Joseph Bentley Leyland (1888–1969),
who dedicated his life to making West Vancouver a place where
future generations would like to live.

TABLE OF CONTENTS

Opposite: A house perches on dramatic terrain in Caulfeild Plateau.

Photo by John Moir

Background: An architect's models enable clients to visualize complex designs on rugged coastal terrain.

Photos of models courtesy Barry Griblin

Perched like a mountainside lodge, the Cianci house, designed by German architect Hanns Carl Berchtenbreiter in 1933, embodies the European aesthetic associated with the "design with nature" movement that would influence West Coast Modern architects in the following decades.

Photo by John Moir

PREFACE

> A city is for the safety and convenience of its citizens and the surprise and delight of strangers.
>
> —Architect Sansovia, ca. 1500

West Vancouver's narrow band of population unfurls across the North Shore from Capilano River to Horseshoe Bay, backed by a rugged mountainous wilderness, blessed by a benign climate, warmed (when it's not raining) by the southern sun. Illustrating the dictum of the Canadian poet Irving Layton, "geography is fate," its rugged terrain, physical separation and proximity to a large urban centre have shaped its development.

West Vancouver is (to the best of local knowledge) the only south-facing residential community in the northern hemisphere that overlooks a body of water and a major city. North Vancouver, it is true, has a similar setting, but its heavily industrialized waterfront has shaped it in different

An early-morning runner in John Lawson Park. *Photo by John Moir*

Carmichael house, 1957. Ron Thom, architect. *Photo by urbanpictures.com, 2013*

ways. West Vancouver is characterized by magnificent (and expensive) homes and an absence of industry. But it was not always so. In the early years of the past century, visiting Vancouverites enjoyed it as a low-cost vacation destination. They pitched their tents or built their shacks along the beach each summer, returning to their urban life in the fall.

How did West Vancouver get from there to here? This book approaches the question primarily through looking at the issues that surround land—who owns it, who wants it and what gets put on it. Pivotal players include the Squamish people of Capilano Reserve No. 5, whose ancestors have lived on the land for millennia, and British Pacific Properties (BPP, or British Properties), which has gone through many iterations over the past eighty years to arrive at its current proposals for Cypress Village on the western reaches of its property. Many others have brought their own agendas to bear on the land. This book cannot discuss all of the multitudes of development projects, but will trace trends that illuminate the larger patterns. Rather than a traditional history, the following chapters comprise essays probing some of the essential aspects that have formed West Vancouver and will shape its future.

Many dedicated community builders have brought their clearly defined vision to the community. They haven't always enjoyed success, and their visions have not all withstood the test of time, but they've all been motivated by a genuine desire to make this community a better place. John Lawson, Francis Caulfeild, Joseph Leyland, Roy Pidgeon, Claire Downing, Perry Willoughby and Heinz Berger are some of the more important dreamers and designers who poured their energy and often substantial amounts of their own resources into making the municipality a place where its residents now enjoy an unusual quality of life. This book is dedicated to them.

Town and country *must be married*, and out of this joyous union will spring a new hope, a new life, a new civilization.

—Ebenezer Howard, *Garden Cities*

Long before Richard Florida coined the phrase "creative class," West Vancouver's isolation and dramatic terrain have been a haven for artists and entrepreneurs. Since 1938, the Lions Gate Bridge has been both a link to Vancouver and a symbol of the distinct character of the North Shore in general, and West Van in particular.

Photo by John Moir

INTRODUCTION

LIFE ON THE TIP OF A SPIKY WORLD

In *Who's Your City,* urbanist Richard Florida argues that we are living in a "spiky world," in which about two dozen locations dominate the global economy through their economic activity, creativity and innovation. These cities and urban regions feed on their success, as the presence of the best and brightest attracts more of their colleagues for the lucrative, challenging jobs and quality of life on offer, generating a synergy that fosters dynamic communities. He represents these on a map in which the tallest spikes indicate the most intense concentrations. Creativity, innovation and economic productivity concentrate particularly in Tokyo, San Francisco, New York and Seoul. Vancouver is in the vanguard, along with cities like Toronto, Paris, Stockholm and Taipei. West Vancouver, with its spectacular geography and splendid layout, is one of the most desirable (spikiest?) communities in the desirable Lower Mainland.

Florida demonstrates that the lure of high income is not the only or even the main reason a given city attracts people. "The higher people rate the beauty of their community, its physical environment, and recreational offerings, the higher their overall level of community satisfaction."[1] All Lower Mainland communities are blessed by nature, but West Vancouver is arguably the most so. Its geography—bordered on three sides by water with a backdrop of wilderness on the north, threaded by multiple creeks and cleft by ravines that provide endless avenues to natural enjoyment—gives it a distinct identity. The larger setting provides opportunities for unparalleled outdoor activity—mountain biking, skiing, hiking, sailing, you name it—complementing cultural amenities that provide opportunities for a rich and satisfying life. A cosmopolitan and educated citizenry provides possibilities for stimulating personal contacts.

Results of computer analysis by Chanuki Seresinhe and her colleagues at the Warwick Business School on what makes a landscape scenic and attractive have borne out Florida's findings, giving them greater specificity. "Lakes and horizons scored well. So did valleys and snowy mountains . . . Hospitals, garages and motels not so much . . . Green spaces are not, in and of themselves scenic. To be so they need to involve contours and trees."[2] West Vancouver, anyone?

In looking more closely at Florida's argument, it becomes clear that the Lower Mainland's attractiveness as a place to live and work far outweighs its importance as a contributor to the global economy. Compared with cities like Beijing or Shanghai, the quality of life in Vancouver, particularly West Vancouver, is much higher, even though its economic and innovative clout is far less. Few if any cities in the world can match the ambience of excellent skiing less than a half-hour away from the urban centre, followed by the relaxing beauty of a sunset walk on the seawall. But its modest accomplishments in innovative technology have made it a place where salaries are less of an attraction than its high quality of life. Vancouver's attractive physical setting and benign weather have fostered a demand for housing that has sent prices far beyond the affordability of most of its residents.

British cultural traditions laid West Vancouver's foundations. The urban squalor of nineteenth-century industrial cities, particularly London, deeply concerned many, from the poet William Blake on through social critic John Ruskin to Ebenezer Howard, the English founder of the "garden city" movement. Jobs attracted huge numbers of workers to London and other industrial cities, creating horrific slums. Howard aimed to reduce the alienation of humans and society from nature through the creation of ideal communities that incorporated the natural world. He expressed his utopian but practical views in *To-morrow: A Peaceful Path to Reform* (1898), revised and reissued as *Garden Cities of To-morrow* in 1902. As eminent sociologist Lewis Mumford noted in his introduction to the later book, what was needed was "a marriage of town and country, of rustic health and sanity, and activity and urban knowledge, urban technical facility, urban political co-operation."[3] Howard collaborated in the creation of Letchworth, near London, the world's first garden city, in 1904, where the restorative powers of the natural world softened the hard edges of urban life. Letchworth continues today.

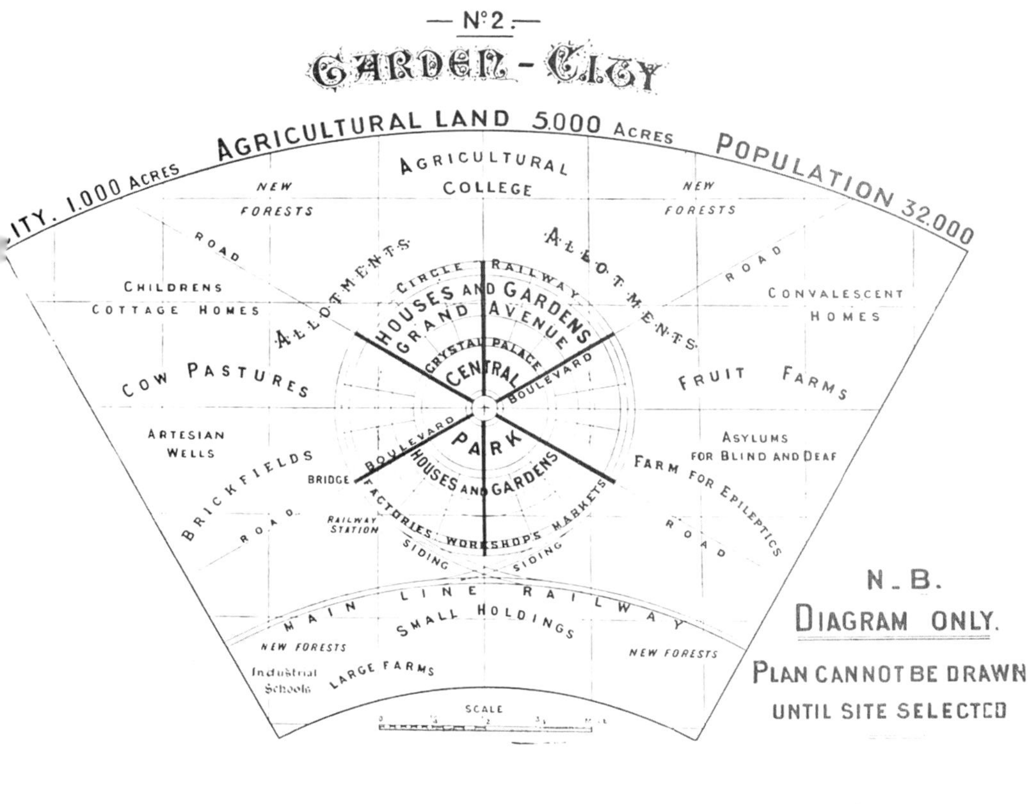

Ebenezer Howard's schematics for garden cities were pleasingly symmetrical, if naively idealistic, giving promise for a balanced way of life. *Reprinted from Ebenezer Howard,* Garden Cities of To-morrow *(London, 1902). From Wikimedia Commons*

> I will not cease from
> Mental Flight,
> Nor shall my sword sleep
> in my hand:
> Till we have built
> Jerusalem,
> In England's green &
> pleasant land.
> —William Blake

The absence of industrial ills in West Vancouver meant few man-made barriers existed to creating the kind of community Howard considered ideal, and many were motivated not to repeat the mistakes made elsewhere. A succession of pioneers drew on Howard's ideas in developing the North Shore. He may have been part of the inspiration for the grandiose Grand Boulevard in North Vancouver, built in 1908: one of the main streets in Howard's proposed garden city was a 420-foot (127-metre) wide Grand Avenue. And he was almost certainly in the mind of Francis Caulfeild, who in 1899 and 1900 acquired nearly a thousand acres of rugged coastal land east of Horseshoe Bay.

Caulfeild hailed from Clovelly in North Devon, England, a privately owned town now famous for its steep cobbled streets, picturesque beauty

Two graciously dressed women, probably members of the Kilby family, pick wildflowers along a path in Caulfeild. No hardy pioneers, the Kilbys were comfortably off Vancouver home-furnishing merchants, and used their home in Caulfeild as a summer retreat, living their ideal of the romantic English country life in West Vancouver. *West Vancouver Museum and Archives, 1883.2.WVA.RAH*

and absence of cars. His family had a long and respected lineage: Sir Toby Caulfeild sailed with Francis Drake against the Spanish Armada; three centuries later, Francis Caulfeild, who graduated from the prestigious Rugby School in Warwickshire and from Wadham College, Oxford, and later became manager of Lloyds Bank of London, looked for new challenges across the ocean. His literary interests included a translation of *The Odyssey*, parts of which he read at a meeting of Canadian authors on his property. Perhaps he saw himself as a modern-day Ulysses, questing for Ithaca as he contended with difficulties in the course of his epic journey.

In his new home Caulfeild implemented his utopian vision, one driven more by aesthetics and ideology than financial speculation, although he financed his enterprise by selling lots. He laid out streets in apparently haphazard fashion based, he said, on cowpaths. These lend a natural charm that endures today. "It is," he was fond of saying, "the business of the man not to despise the wisdom of the cow, but to graft upon it the fruits of his own science and experience." A cow belonging to the local pilot assistant, Tom Grafton, known to trample Caulfeild's flowers in its quest for the best path, was a good test of Caulfeild's theories—and his patience.

Caulfeild found the way local Vancouver real estate relied on "nothing but a T-Square" appalling. In a short article, "The Philosophy of Town Planning," he laid out his alternate vision. "From an aesthetic point of view nothing can be more hopelessly unsatisfactory than the rectangular system." The justification goes beyond aesthetic to social considerations. Anticipating the modernist architects of a half century later, he wrote that if every house and every street were like its neighbour, the sameness would make excellence unfamiliar and cramp the imaginations of its residents. His vision for West Vancouver was aided by the terrain, the rugged contours of which made straight lines all but impossible.

He would have been aware of Frederick Olmsted, often considered the father of American landscape architecture, or a "landscape gardener," as he preferred to call himself. Olmsted had designed Montreal's Mount Royal, New York's Central Park, the grounds of the White House and many other North American urban landscapes. Like Caulfeild, he encouraged "the full utilization of the naturally occurring features of a given space." He believed that scenery worked through an unconscious process to relax faculties experiencing tension as a result of the noise and artificial surroundings of urban life. His sons' company, the Olmsted

Brothers, continued their father's work and would be hired in 1933 to design the initial phase of the British Properties.

Although similarities existed between Caulfeild's vision and that of Frederick Olmsted and his sons, their respective West Vancouver developments differ. Although it might be argued that Caulfeild's work, embodying his respect for the landscape's contours, serves as a prototype for the early development of the British Properties with its streets contoured to the geography, his vision was nineteenth-century romantic, working sensitively with the land at hand. The properties, with their array of covenants shaping the nature of their development, allowed less room for personal indulgence. No doubt Caulfeild benefited from having a comparatively small area to manage rather than the thousands of acres of the properties, but driving or walking through each of these residential areas makes for a vastly different experience: where Caulfeild resembles an intimate walk down an English village lane, the British Properties, its name notwithstanding, typifies an attempt to realize the American Dream. Not many walkers here. Caulfeild conceived his development before cars shaped our society, whereas the British Properties assumed the necessity of car ownership and use.

The dream of an ideal community that combined the finest of Western civilization and human endeavour with the beauty of nature has never been far in the background of West Vancouver's development. Perhaps a new Athens of the north? It's intriguing that one of West Vancouver's most famous buildings replicated the Parthenon, and where else is there a better natural Acropolis than the former Parthenon's location on the craggy cliffs of Eagle Harbour?

Until 1926 West Vancouver's development took place with little municipal control. In that year, Town Zoning Bylaw 308 pointed West Vancouver to a future of single-family homes of a suitably respectable nature. That future has now been tempered with several realities: lack of space for single-family homes, their extravagant cost and the need for higher density to generate the taxes needed for urban infrastructure. Joseph "Joe" Leyland, elected to council in 1926 and reeve from 1930 to 1940, played a pivotal role in moving West Vancouver from a summer beachfront of largely temporary residents toward a community of mostly upscale homes. He fought vigorously to implement the infrastructure, particularly the Lions Gate Bridge, needed to meet this goal. The zoning he promoted helped prevent the worst sins of urban sprawl but, as West

Vancouver developed, those same zoning laws would limit economic diversity. Those on the lower end of the economic scale would often find West Vancouver beyond their means.

The other major players in the planning dialogue have been the British Properties and the Squamish people of Capilano Reserve No. 5. BPP worked hand in glove with the municipality, but both saw the Squamish people more as an inconvenient roadblock than a people with their own rights. In 1931, BPP paid the municipality a paltry $75,000 for 4,000 acres of some of the most magnificent property anywhere, stretching across the North Shore from the Capilano River to Horseshoe Bay, mostly above what is now the Upper Levels Highway. The gradually emerging imprint of their vision on this land has done much to shape West Vancouver. Unlike Shaughnessy and other Lower

Originally conceived as traditional English country estates, the British Properties, after the Second World War, took a decided turn toward North American modernism: expansive, streamlined and centred on the automobile way of life. Elegant realtor Muriel May is standing next to the car on Taylor Way in 1950. *West Vancouver Museum and Archives, 0659.WVA.RAH. Eric Cable photo*

Mainland developments—including West Vancouver's Altamont, where the mansions repose sedately behind manicured lawns in well-treed seclusion—the British Properties' achievements are clearly visible to all who cross the Lions Gate Bridge or drive the properties' streets.

The Squamish people of Capilano Reserve should have been key players, but until fairly recently their existence was, at best, barely acknowledged. The reserve sits on 1.7 square kilometres of land on the north shore of the First Narrows, a tiny (but significant) area compared with West Vancouver's 87.1 square kilometres. For many years, successive governments and businesses from West Vancouver and elsewhere have attempted to marginalize them by plundering their ancestral home for its land and resources. Despite over a century of neglect and mistreatment, however, the Squamish have frequently asserted their rights. Since about 1970, more of their efforts have met with success. In 1983, they won the battle to have the lands south of the Park Royal Mall, which had been severed from the reserve by the McKenna-McBride Commission in 1916, returned to them.

BPP is a private company that must abide by municipal bylaws, whereas the Squamish establish and administer regulations relevant to their community. As a result, the Squamish can now develop their land in ways they believe will further the well-being of their people without reference to municipal bylaws or development plans. The municipality, however, can exert considerable leverage through the building (or not) of roads and other infrastructure such as water and sewage lines.

Not surprisingly, dialogue among the Squamish, BPP and the municipality has often been hampered by conflicting objectives. Much of the evolution of West Vancouver and the Capilano Reserve has focused on struggles for control of the land where the three have interacted. Lions Gate Bridge traffic enters and leaves the bridge on land severed from the reserve. In 1950, just to the west of the bridge, BPP built the initial phase of Park Royal Shopping Centre on land leased from Capilano Reserve to facilitate the marketing of their estates a short drive up the mountain slope. The evolving interface of these different agendas provides fascinating insights into the dynamics that have shaped this community.

The impetus for growth in West Vancouver, largely driven by developers, realtors and their eager clientele, has often been opposed by those who fear the effects of change. Although many new projects are underway and being planned, population growth in West Vancouver for

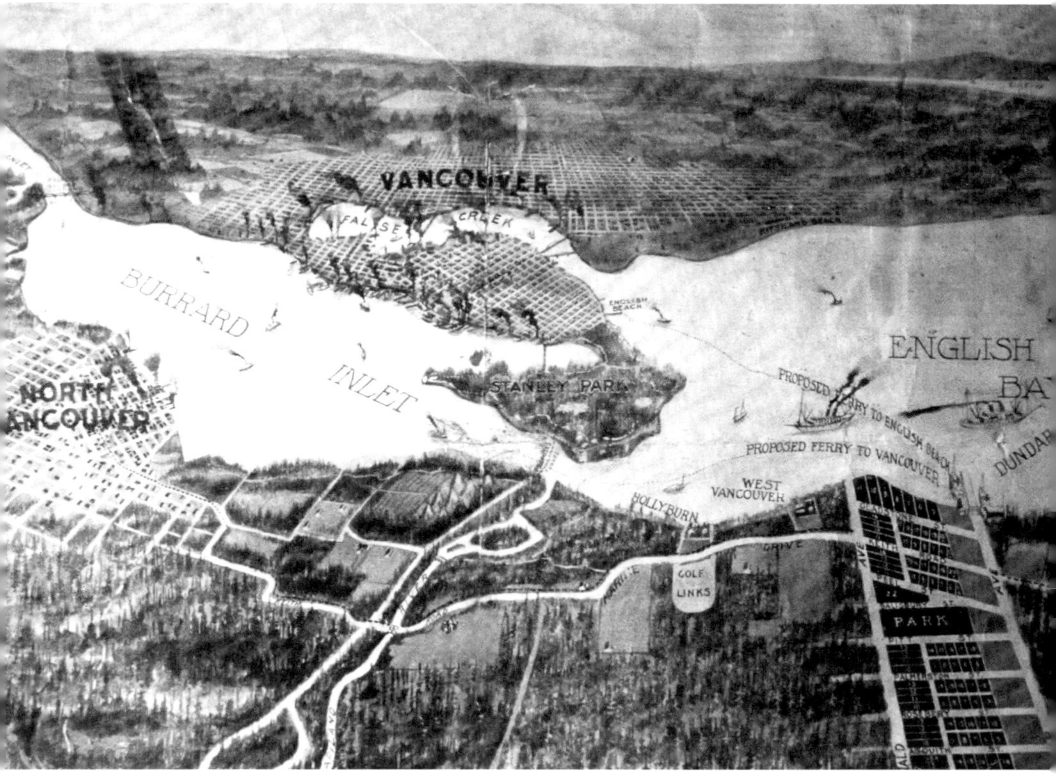

This inventive, if imprecise, 1911 illustration shows a proposal for an outsized subdivision in Dundarave. Imaginative North Van realtors Irwin and Billings even include a proposed tunnel under the First Narrows for easy access to West Van.
West Vancouver Memorial Library, 0916.CC

the past thirty years has remained considerably below projections, and in recent years has declined slightly. Increased ethnic diversity is bringing a richer flavour to community life, although not without substantial stress to the community fabric.

The history of West Vancouver has played out on a backdrop of freedom versus control. Caulfeild believed in allowing a high degree of freedom in his original development, although later expressions of freedom, such as the building of ostentatious mansions, demonstrate a downside of this approach. The more controlled approaches of Leyland and the British Properties in its earlier years prevented unchecked growth, but limited diversity and individual spontaneity. Similarly, the goal has

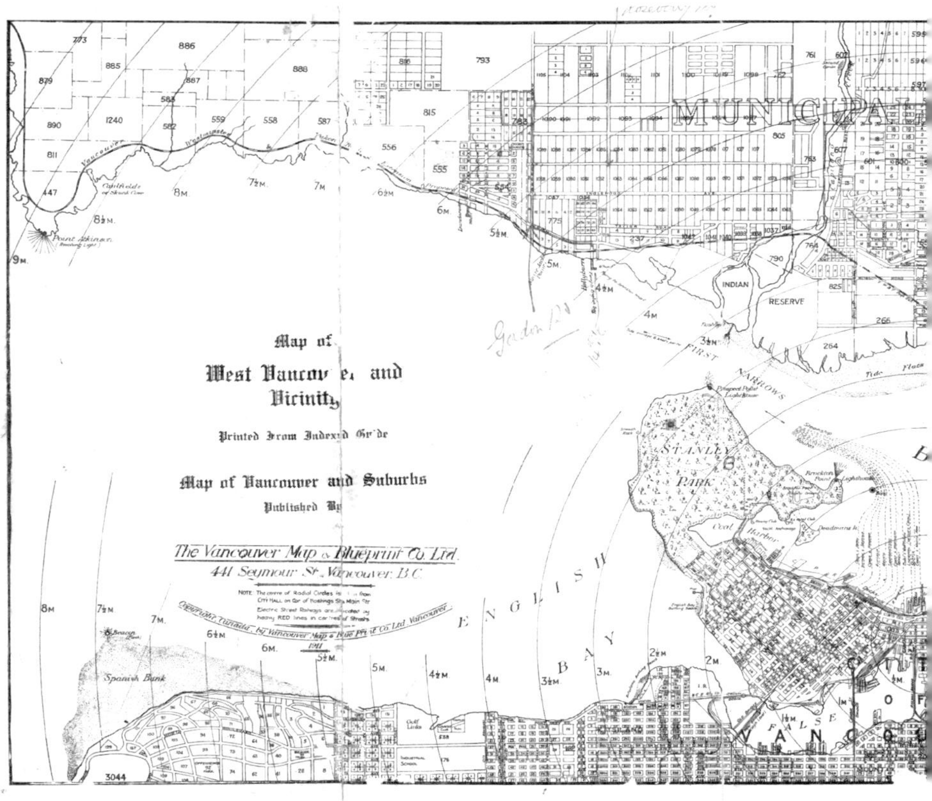

often been to control the people of Capilano Reserve No. 5, but these efforts have typically done more to hinder than help progress that might benefit both communities. The interaction between control and freedom continues to characterize much of West Vancouver's development. How can desires for individual freedom be balanced against the good of the community?

Richard Florida breaks down the contemporary workforce into four classes: creative, service, manufacturing and agricultural. West Vancouver is home to a large number of people from the creative class, both currently working and retired, who Florida loosely defines as professional people: the managerial class, knowledge workers and medical workers. This group, which has the highest income, has grown in North America from 5 per cent in 1900 to about 10 per cent in 1950 and about 30 per cent today. It will likely continue to grow, while the agricultural and manufacturing sectors have and probably will continue to decline

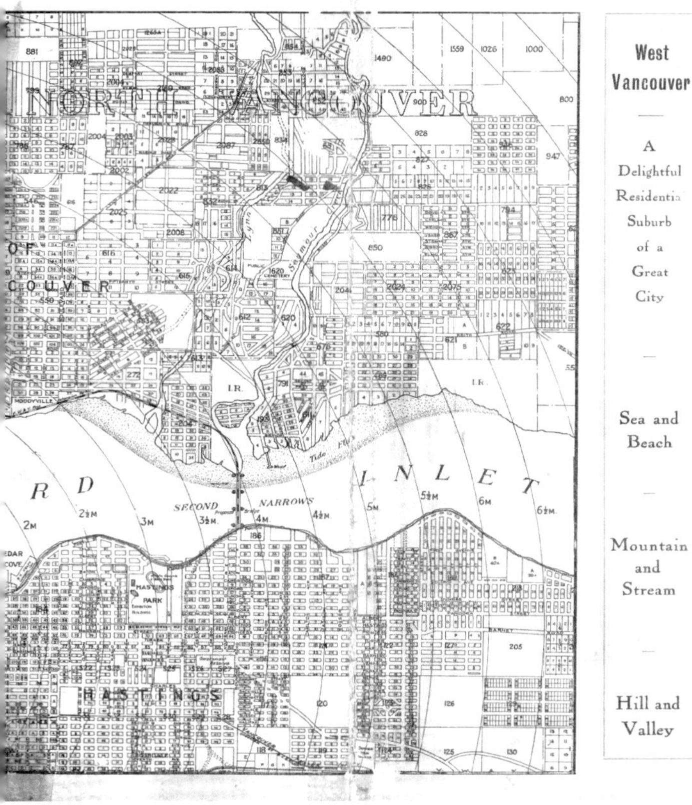

This 1911 map of West Vancouver and Vicinity shows an orderly grid for the layout of West Vancouver. Over time, these plans for lots and streets, as well as a proposed railway running through the heart of Lighthouse Park, would undergo many changes as the facts of politics and terrain came into play. The radiating lines indicate the distance from Vancouver City Hall, then at Hastings and Main Street. *City of Vancouver Archives LEG1340.1*

sharply. The low-paid service class, comprising baristas, caregivers, store workers and others, has also increased, and is now at about 45 per cent in North American society. Although they are at the bottom of the economic heap, these people are essential to the functioning of any community.

However, although West Vancouver's attractiveness as a place to live is undeniable, even well-paid members of the creative class often have difficulty moving here. Few rentals are available and the price of houses has reached stratospheric heights, averaging $3.1 million in 2017. The price of housing forces many of those who work here to commute long distances, causing problems that range from minor (some restaurants have limited hours because staff are not available) to potentially life-threatening (a natural disaster could be doubly disastrous in a city whose first responders mostly live elsewhere). Designing a community that works for all its residents is an increasing challenge.

Would you assist me in ensuring that West Vancouver retains its attractiveness by insisting that your tenants do not make the balconies a laundry area and at the same time do have some co-ordination of both colour and design of screening materials [on their balconies]...

—A letter from West Vancouver mayor Derrick Humphreys to apartment building owners, May 1, 1983

This 1923 map of West Van shows how place names change over time. For example, what is now Sentinel Hill was Baby Mountain and what was then Eagle Harbour became what is now Fisherman's Cove. To confuse the issue further, Eagle Harbour would later move itself a little to the east, sending Shelter Bay to oblivion.

City of Vancouver Archives, AM1594-: MAP 302

01

THE STRUGGLE FOR BALANCE

FREEDOM AND CONTROL

Zoning developed in the nineteenth century to foster better living conditions, at least for the middle class. Zoning separated the dirt and noise of factories from the cleanliness and order of middle-class residential developments as much as possible. Ebenezer Howard was an early promoter of zoning in his English garden-city plans at the turn of the last century. From 1916 North American cities began to create living patterns that would lead to more humane living conditions; zoning was a way of keeping like things together, whether residential, commercial or industrial.

From the beginning, many recognized that diversity was often a casualty of zoning, necessary though it might be. Well-known urbanist Jane Jacobs was not a fan: "the greatest flaw in city zoning is that it permits monotony."[4] Control of development has often conflicted with the freedom many desire to pursue individual aesthetic and financial goals. Modernist architects after the Second World War, for example, had difficulty getting mortgages because the Canadian Mortgage and Housing Corporation (CMHC) did not like the flat roofs that most modernist houses featured. How can a community control the negative effects of growth and development while allowing its residents the freedom to indulge their imaginations and their own personal bent?

Although West Vancouver's industrial ills were minimal, zoning provided a way of implementing controls that would forestall urban problems before they started. Until the 1920s, West Vancouver served mainly as a summer playground for Vancouverites, who enjoyed a laid-back lifestyle in their summer tents and shacks—the hippies of an earlier age, who lived without the constraints imposed elsewhere. As the municipality grew in the '20s, with less room for wandering cows and eccentrics, much of the quirky diversity of the early years yielded to the interests of those who wished a more organized and permanent community. Some of the less socially or economically advantaged residents either stayed away or left.

Joseph Bentley Leyland and His Vision

> Few indeed are but thrilled at the panoramic views to be had from any point of vantage, over-looking lovely bays, rocky cliffs rising sheer from the water's edge, and beautiful islands like huge waves swaying lazily on the bosom of the Pacific.
>
> —Joseph Leyland in the *West Vancouver News*, July 26, 1929

Surrounded by a swirl of Union Jack flags, Reeve Joseph Leyland presides at the opening of the Capilano Bridge in 1930. Eight years later he would be opening the proud accomplishment of the Lions Gate Bridge. *West Vancouver Museum and Archives, 120.WVA.LEY*

In 1925 the provincial government's Town Planning Act gave BC cities certain powers of zoning and restrictions. West Vancouver, under Reeve David Morgan, quickly seized the opportunity with a 1926 town planning bylaw (Bylaw 308) that "declared that the presence of tents, huts or shacks . . . reduce the value of the assessable property . . . and—or are unsanitary." This bylaw regulated the use and location of buildings and land, leading to the division of West Vancouver into districts: Ambleside, Dundarave, Caulfeild and Horseshoe Bay. Councillor Joseph "Joe" Leyland, who shared responsibility for the bylaw with municipal solicitor Gordon Robson, saw the problem as not only the shacks themselves but the seasonal nature of West Vancouver's population, which hindered the creation of a year-round community.

Leyland, West Vancouver's man of the half century (1900–50), was the most prominent of the second wave of West Vancouver's community builders, people who built on the groundwork laid by Francis Caulfeild, John Lawson and others. He focused with unrelenting energy on developing his community, doing more than anyone else to develop West Vancouver into a unified city. But he had his contradictions. His ardent support of North America's democratic and egalitarian spirit did nothing to dampen his enthusiastic support of the Guinnesses (the famed brewing dynasty) and the British Properties. And while he worked to make West Vancouver a community of upscale single-family residences, he lived his own life in a modest waterfront home next to Rodgers Creek, taking in boarders and renting adjacent cottages to augment his family's income.

Joseph Bentley Leyland was born in England on January 11, 1888, the younger of two sons of John (1857–1924) and Fanny Julia (1847–1921). The Leyland family traces its origins to the Norman Conquest, when William the Conqueror bestowed on them the area now known as the town of Leyland in county Lancashire. Three Leylands fought on the side of Henry V at the Battle of Agincourt. In the latter part of the seventeenth century, the remaining branches of the family moved to Yorkshire, where many distinguished themselves in art, science and literature.

Leyland's grandfather, Francis Alexander Leyland (1813–94), was an antiquarian, printer and bookseller, and authority on medieval art; he designed the Halifax (England) coat of arms. Francis Leyland's older brother and Reeve Leyland's namesake, Joseph Bentley Leyland (1811–51) was a talented sculptor, painter, poet and a friend of Branwell Brontë, brother to the famous Brontë sisters, and his frequent drinking partner at the George Hotel or one of a number of other establishments. Here their literary group met to discuss their writing and enjoy convivial times. Francis Leyland's two-volume biography of the Brontës, *The Brontë Family, with Special Reference to Patrick Branwell Brontë* (1883), attempted to rehabilitate the image of the ill-fated Branwell, who ruined his life with drugs and alcohol, as described in Elizabeth Gaskell's biography of Charlotte Brontë. The older Joseph Leyland's own life was also marred by dependence on drugs and alcohol. He died in debtors' prison, but his brother Francis remained faithful to him to the end.

The younger Joe's father, John Leyland, was a well-known naval expert and authority on international affairs, with diverse literary and artistic interests. Like his son, he was a great doer. His numerous publications include a number of books on local history such as *The Peak of Derbyshire: Its Scenery and Antiquities* (1891), *Thames Illustrated: A Picturesque Journeying from Richmond to Oxford* (1900), *Gardens, Old and New: The Country House and its Garden Environment* (1902) and *The Shakespeare Country Illustrated* (1909). His books on naval issues include such titles as *Dispatches and Letters Relating to the Blockade of Brest* (2 volumes) and *The Royal Navy, Its Influence on English History and the Growth of the Empire*, which was the authoritative manual on British naval history. He devoted much of his writing to educating the public on the necessity of maintaining and increasing the navy's efficiency. On his death, *The Times*, to which he contributed frequently, praised his "erudition and judgement . . . combined with a style which was illuminating and persuasive." On a more personal note, his son Joe describes him as "Always tolerant and forgiving of others, he was the essence of modesty, and often oblivious of self; his capacious appetite for knowledge was combined with an insatiable desire to keep busy in doing good for others."

Joe Leyland received a good education at a private school and St. Mary's College, a Benedictine boarding school. At St. Mary's, he joined the Douai Literary and Debating Society; in 1905, he presented a well-received paper on "The British Navy." He left before the end of his final year to sit the rigorous civil service examinations, which he passed, for an assistant clerkship in the Royal Navy. His father might have hoped that he would join the navy or attend a good university such as Oxford or Cambridge. Perhaps not wishing either (he was prone to seasickness), he chose instead to immigrate to Canada.

Leyland arrived in Canada on St. Patrick's Day in 1905 at the age of seventeen, with forty dollars in his pocket. His father had arranged for him to work at Poplar Glen farm in Manitou, Manitoba, earning sixty dollars for the year—demanding work, but he did not succumb to his parents' suggestions to return home, preferring the freedom to pursue his dreams. Work followed as a subscription agent for the Winnipeg *Telegram* in Portage la Prairie and as a bookkeeper, first in future prime minister Arthur Meighen's law office, then in the office of E.A. McPherson, later Chief Justice for Manitoba. In 1907 he began work in Winnipeg for the Great West Life Assurance Company, through which he met and, in 1914, married Margaretta (Etta) Barber of Regina.

But he had not yet found his place. In letters to his father in the early '20s, an ambitious Leyland lamented that "my career in Canada has just been 'average' and 'ordinary,'" although he appreciated the North American "elimination of class distinctions and equal opportunities for all": "The absence of overcrowded cities, slums and poverty, the real democratic freedom of the West, the feeling that one is unfettered by class distinctions and increasing competition, has all given one opportunities of advancement and independence not to be found in England." The destiny of Canada, he felt, lay both geographically and economically with its neighbours to the south. "I have not the least hesitation in believing that in the not too distant future, there will be one country from the Panama Canal to the Arctic."

In other letters, he tempered his enthusiasm for the American model with an awareness of the values of British ties and the desirability of an independent Canada. "My own personal desire would be to see Canada a new and separate independent Nation, living in permanent peace with both England and the United States." His head connected him to the US, but England stirred his heart.

He had visited Vancouver in his travels across Canada for his insurance work and, after a honeymoon visit in 1914, he and his wife decided that the West Coast was where they would like to settle. They arrived in 1917 with their two-year-old daughter Josie, and after a year in Vancouver's West End they moved to West Vancouver, initially sharing the top floor of the Clachan in Dundarave with Edie Kemp and her daughter Bea. They also lived for a time in the nearby Fortune Cup, built in 1919, and later for a short period in a small cottage in Altamont. They built a two-bedroom cottage on the West Vancouver waterfront at Rodgers Creek.

In their new homes, they raised their two children: Josephine (born in 1915) and John (born in 1922).

Josie described summer pleasures in her charming memoir: "At the mouth of the stream there was a waterfall about five feet high, formed by an immense fallen tree where the stream poured into the sea, and at the bottom there was a pool about two feet deep. We used to fish for little trout with a bent pin on the end of a string, with no great success… In the winter time the stream was a raging torrent. We would hear the huge rocks rolling around…In summer the water was quite low and we had a box down in the stream in which we kept our milk, butter, etc." Excursions included trips to Sandy Cove or Caulfeilds Beach. "On the way home we would stop at the cannery and buy a salmon, for 25c! Sometimes we would hike from Caulfeilds out to Point Atkinson Light House where Mr. Grafton, the lighthouse keeper, in his slow drawl would tell us all about the light and how it worked."

This was an idyllic place where nature displayed an unusual beauty, which Joe deeply appreciated. "The sunsets, looking across the Straits to Vancouver Island are often inspiring—the most beautiful Moving Picture in the world. After a heavy rain our stream is also a thing of beauty, with a Falls like a young Niagara—it is interesting in the season to see the salmon trying to jump up the Falls. Little did I ever think we would live in such a spot." His granddaughter Dorothy described "him combing the beach every day after the tide had gone out, wearing a heavy plaid shirt with the sleeves rolled up, and carrying a bushel basket so that he could harvest the most recent pieces of driftwood that had been carried in with the tide the night before. This catch was then carefully sorted (bark, timber, logs, sticks, etc.), stacked and stored. The large pieces were added to the already great, long rows of wood stacked along the outer edge of the garden toward the sea, serving as an extra breakwater from the high tides and the crashing waves that occurred once in a while." Leyland's other pleasures included playing tennis, golf or bridge, smoking an occasional cigar, and having vigorous political conversations with family and friends. He slept outside on the veranda most of the year, his loud snoring blending with the sounds of the waves breaking on shore, and the melodious Rodgers Creek flowing past their house.

Leyland's long absences from the family, due to his heavy travelling schedule for the insurance company, left running the home and raising the children in their early years mostly to his wife Etta. She did much to enhance the quality of their life, sewing nearly all the children's clothes and taking in a number of boarders throughout and after the Depression. During the Second World War she worked at Burrard Dry Dock's pay office in North Vancouver. As they had little money to hire any help, she did many of the repairs on the house herself. She managed their rental cottages on the western side of the creek, and was a wonderful cook and hostess. She was vice president of the PTA and belonged to the Imperial Order Daughters of the Empire (IODE), every year hosting afternoon teas and the IODE garden party.

The Leyland waterfront home, a modest two-bedroom cottage located on Bellevue at the mouth of Rodgers Creek, was the site of many family and community gatherings. *West Vancouver Museum and Archives, 150.WVA.LEY*

When Leyland's father died in early 1924, he sailed to England on the *Aquitania* to wrap up his estate. He described meeting a number of wealthy and cultured fellow passengers, often expressing feelings of inadequacy concerning his lack of similar education and wealth. "They realize my opportunities have been limited, and are well bred enough to be very sociable, and have made the trip very pleasant for me indeed." Much of his drive to become successful was likely motivated by an awareness of his family's illustrious ancestors and a desire to acquit himself honourably.

Mrs. Leyland and their two young children later sailed to England on the *Antonia*, where they joined husband and father in England and lived there for the better part of a year. In their absence, their West Vancouver cottage burned down, so after their return on the *Mauritania* they bought two dilapidated houses on the other side of Rodgers Creek from their burned-out house, which had been used by summer campers. On one of the lots, they built a two-bedroom home, which they named "Crimsworth Dene" after Leyland's childhood home in Forest Hill, London. They renovated and rented one of the shacks; they tore the other down and built a new rentable house on the site. They built another rental home on the site where their own home had burned down.

The Leylands frequently entertained in their new home with a night of music and singing. As Leyland said, "Good music was like wine to the heart and mind." His daughter Josie recalls that "there were quite a number of good voices, including my father," which may have in part been fuelled by the potent beer they brewed in their basement. With additions and renovations, 2848 Bellevue became their home for the next forty years. The current house on this site, built in 1997, was assessed at $18,952,000 in 2017.

Leyland left Great West and started his own insurance business in Vancouver in October 1925. This allowed him to escape the constant travelling, spending more time with his family and immersing himself in West Vancouver community issues. His granddaughter Dorothy wrote that "preservation of the environment, clean air and water, and equal opportunity and justice for all were the values to which he subscribed. Because Canada was a new country, there seemed to be unlimited opportunities to create a new culture and society that no country in Europe could ever imagine." Western Canada, Leyland believed, "was where the true spirit of democracy could be found." His granddaughter Barbara Evans described him as "civic-minded to the core, selling insurance because he had to, but building West Vancouver because he wanted to." He was "as kind a man as I ever met." Dorothy wrote that "local government and participation by the permanent residents really meant something; there were children to teach, town services to provide, and budding new businesses to help establish and serve."

Once Leyland had established his own insurance business in Vancouver, he could take on more leadership roles in his own community. He became president of the West Vancouver Conservative Association, and was elected councillor in January 1926. His numerous civic involvements began with being chairman of finance, fire and publicity in 1926 and of transportation and health in 1927. In 1928 he was elected a member of the school board and chairman of the grounds committee. After an unsuccessful run against V.V. Vinson for the reeveship in 1929, he ran against William James Dent and Robert Fiddes, achieving election on January 18, 1930. He won elections three times, was elected by acclamation eight, and also served as president of the Union of British Columbia Municipalities (UBCM) in 1939.

Leyland loved completing important municipal projects, and felt impatient with bureaucrats and those who placed unnecessary obstacles in his way. He oversaw the building of the steel-trussed Capilano Bridge across the Capilano River at Marine Drive in 1930, which stood for over seventy years. He advocated for building a highway up Howe Sound, seeing West Vancouver as a portal to the development of Garibaldi as a park and tourist centre. He was also a driving force behind the building of Lions Gate Bridge, which gave West Vancouver a reliable road connection to Vancouver.

Throughout his tenure as reeve and beyond, Leyland brought an unflagging energy to his community involvement. His roles were far too numerous to itemize completely here, but the most important included positions as director or chairman from 1931 to 1944 of the forerunner of the British Columbia Automobile Association (BCAA); executive director or chairman from 1941 to 1945 of ten war service campaigns, for which he raised $5.5 million; and vice-president and director from 1942 of the Vancouver Council of Social Agencies. His sporting activities included being founding director and president of the West Vancouver Tennis Club from 1925. Although he did not remain a practising Catholic after his father's death, the family were members of St. Stephen's Anglican Church. He was active in the Freemasons King David's Lodge for forty years.

Unfortunately, his later years were marred by Alzheimer's. On the occasion of his death in 1969, his obituary read in part, "he was a man of strong convictions based on the tenets of true democracy and at the same time showing a dedication to his municipality that has rarely been equalled." His granddaughter Barbara Evans struck a personal note. "At heart, I believe Grandpa was a genuine dreamer." His wife Margaretta passed away in 1973.

The year 1926 was pivotal to West Vancouver's coming of age, with the Second Narrows Bridge providing road access (when not incapacitated by errant ships) from 1925. The Hollyburn Theatre opened in 1926, as did Appleton Court, the first apartment building, located where the municipal hall now stands. Optimism buoyed the community. In the same year, Pacific Stages was granted the right to run buses through West Vancouver over the Second Narrows Bridge. Building permits for the first five months of 1926 totalled $199,685, more than the combined totals of both the City and District of North Vancouver. The population had mushroomed from a mere 700 at incorporation in 1912 to 7,000 in 1926. After this time it slowed markedly, with only 7,500 living here in 1938.

Journalist E.H. Scott expressed the enthusiasm many felt: "In one year West Vancouver has been placed 'on the map' as one of the most progressive municipalities in Greater Vancouver. . . . From what was looked on as a summer resort in the spring of 1925, this seaside beauty spot has become a thriving town." Local Caulfeild resident Julia Henshaw took an even more romantic view. "In this year of 1926 many houses, for the most part red-roofed wooden cottages, whose shingles glow like cornelias in the deep green setting of conifers and arbutus trees fringe the shore; their gay gardens sweeping down over the cliffs in a series of terraces and pockets."[5]

Although zoning lends itself less readily to picturesque language, Leyland saw it as necessary tough love, crucial to guiding the development of his community. It protected property values, controlling the height, setbacks and overall square footage of a house or lot, but not the type or character of building construction. Although necessary, it spelled the eventual end of the Huck Finn existence that his and many other families had enjoyed on the waterfront. The monotony that urbanist Jane Jacobs had decried was not entirely escaped, but a community can't remain static.

When Leyland became reeve in 1930, he introduced a town planning policy that confirmed West Vancouver as a residential area with zoning, building, plumbing and other regulations and bylaws clearly outlined. The main intent was to eliminate the tents and shacks from the waterfront, which did not fit with council's aspiration for West Vancouver to become an upscale year-round residential community. No doubt its summer visitors did not always take responsibility for their space. Vancouver archivist Major Matthews found that Hollyburn "is somewhat the worse

Like many newcomers in the early 1900s, the Reid family made do with a tent, this one set up on the corner of a lot near 14th and Esquimalt. If their dwelling was humble, the Reids could at least take pride in a flourishing garden. *West Vancouver Memorial Library, 1626.WVML*

for wear; the fences down, the tennis court a patchwork of dried grass and dust holes in which children play with sand, a plentiful scattering of cigarettes, boxes, empty lunch papers, and other debris of picnics."[6]

Leyland himself found the washing being hung out by the residents at East Beach (in Ambleside) disturbing as he passed by on the ferry. A half century later, Derrick Humphreys (see epigraph to this chapter) similarly objected to apartment owners hanging laundry off their balconies. Leyland had the council declare the beachfront a park and by the mid-'30s eviction notices were served to those in a number of waterfront cottages, directing them to vacate their property by April 1, 1935. Many of the displaced cottagers resented this; one of them, Bill

In the early 1900s, houses around Ambleside's waterfront were makeshift affairs, mainly humble cottages and seasonal tents. *West Vancouver Memorial Library, 0416. WVML*

Leahey, rowed up to Prince Rupert in search of a new home. Some of the cottages' remains were burned in 1936, although others survived behind Peppi's on the western edge of Dundarave until the 1960s.

Zoning bylaw 308 curtailed but did not eliminate industry in West Vancouver, relegating it to supposedly less desirable areas on its eastern fringes. Industry was still permitted in Zone 3, the area "being within District Lot seven hundred and ninety (790) and what is now known as Indian Reserve No. 5." District Lot (D.L.) 790 includes the area immediately north of Capilano Reserve, from Marine Drive north to Capilano River and east to the North Vancouver boundary, much of which is now occupied by Klahanie Park. Some light industry, particularly gravel removal, took place near the Capilano River. Farther west, the Great Northern Cannery continued operating until calls for its closure were finally heeded in 1967.

The *Vancouver Sun* praised Leyland for sponsoring the town planning policy. "He foresaw the benefits which would accrue and has since worked hard to bring them to fruition."[7] Romantic visionary Francis Caulfeild had been less enthusiastic, expressing his reservations to Councillor Leyland in a letter dated July 10, 1926, regarding the original bylaw. "I am not sure it does not err on the side of entering rather too much into individual detail, and so cramping individual tastes which tends to dullness and monotony."

He disliked the stipulation that it be unlawful to "repair or maintain a building,"[8] the municipality's subtle way of ensuring shacks or tents would inevitably disappear, as without maintenance they would fall into disrepair and eventually need to be demolished.

This polite disagreement between Caulfeild and Leyland on the limits of freedom pointed to different visions of West Vancouver that remain a context for new development. Although Caulfeild's philosophy and motivations radically differed from the more profit-focused priorities of most later developers, he shared with them a desire to allow space for the personal and eccentric. Leyland, on the other hand, was more concerned with the long view, establishing parameters that would channel development and keep West Vancouver primarily a single-home residential community, displaying a consistent and pleasing appearance.

Caulfeild incorporated gennels (paths between houses) in his development, which fostered interaction among residents. These provided public access between individual lots abutting different streets, eliminating the need to walk around an entire block to visit your neighbour. Although most of those in Caulfeild have merged into private property, steep stone steps still lead up the hill from St. Francis Church to Marine Drive, and a path from the Highway to Dogwood Lane provides access to the beach. Gennels have helped humanize subsequent development, and are especially useful for providing access along West Vancouver's numerous creeks. Others run from Marine to Haywood in Dundarave, and between Palmerston and Roseberry just west of Marr Creek. More recently, the British Properties has taken similar steps to foster greater community interaction.

Managing Change and Growth

From November 12, 1938, the Lions Gate Bridge provided easier access to West Vancouver, leading to more growth and drawing more realtors and developers to West Vancouver's Planning Commission, no doubt with dreams of lucrative projects. Further controls respecting the community's welfare were needed to ensure the work of Leyland and others would not disappear into a miasma of tasteless development. Former alderman Ted Baynes noted in "The Dramatic Replanning of West Vancouver in 1944" that, in 1939, "the controls in councils, school boards, planning commissions were in the hands of the local Chamber of Commerce and mainly dominated by the realtors." But a new breed of resident interested in future requirements, such as parks and school sites, also emerged, willing to fight for their vision. Baynes recalled that Reeve Pat Field kicked the realtors off the commission and made sure Roy Pidgeon and Claire Downing were in place to enforce regulated planning to preserve the city's semi-rural charm. At a meeting of the West Vancouver Municipal Affairs Association, Chairman Bob Rolston noted, "I see a couple of realtors in the audience so if they'll please leave we will give them their two dollars back as they go out the door." The realtors stood up and left.[9]

Ed Richardson, who had become municipal engineer in 1940, strongly supported controlled single-family residential planning and was not afraid to act when he perceived the need. As both an engineer and a surveyor, he played a major role in the development of West Vancouver, surveying and overseeing the installation of water, sanitary and storm systems for much of Park Royal, the British Properties and Woodgreen Estates. He was in the unique position of being able to wear one hat to survey a subdivision and then take his plans to the municipality, where he donned another hat and approved them as the municipal engineer. Baynes noted that applications to build shops and small apartments that would have cluttered the landscape "were only stopped because our engineer Ed Richardson always produced the Health Officer to outline the potential problems of sewage disposal." He further said that, until 1944, "zoning was as bad as North Vancouver, with parts of Mathers for local business, and most of Marine Drive destined for pizza or fried chicken huts mixed up with car sales" (with apologies to North Vancouver). Richardson passed away in 2016, still lucid at the age of 107.

> One time Inglewood used to go right through the Pauline Johnson school grounds. Eddie [Richardson] said that's ridiculous—going to kill a kid some day. . . . He took one of the bulldozers and just bulldozed a road around the outside and shut the road off. Nobody saw it in time. It was never dedicated.[10]
>
> —Ted Baynes

In March 1944 Roy Pidgeon, chair of the West Vancouver Planning Commission, argued vigorously and successfully for council to downzone large community-zoned areas of the municipality, particularly Marine Drive, to single-zone use, fostering the development of separate communities, which Leyland had begun in his terms as councillor and reeve. Some sections of the waterfront that had been zoned for apartments were at this time also downzoned to single-family use. Commercial zoning was restricted to areas that were already mostly commercial. The industrial area was even more drastically limited to the southeast corner of Taylor Way and Marine Drive, and Clyde Avenue between 14th and 15th Streets. Wood Products Sash and Door and Western Woodworkers were, at this point, located on the 1400 block of Clyde Avenue.

Pidgeon, with Reeve Pat Fields, Claire Downing and Ed Richardson, were known as "the wise men." Baynes recalls that they "had to fight the press, certain business interests, realtors and some politicians in order to rezone to single-family status." But "He [Pidgeon] had awesome powers to persuade others that he was right."[11]

Harland Bartholomew and Associates was an influential American planning company that had prepared plans for a number of midwest American cities, and in 1928 had laid out a detailed plan for Vancouver. In 1946, along with Vancouver engineer J. Alexander Walker, they prepared a series of six reports for West Vancouver, which have had a strong effect on the city's configuration ever since. Bartholomew saw more rigorous zoning as necessary to establish the size of lots in future subdivisions as a "protection and stabilization of values." According to his vision, streets, transportation, parks, schools, water and so on should precede and govern home construction rather than the reverse. With 95.5 per cent of residential land zoned for single-family homes, West Vancouver's status as a dormitory community for Vancouver appeared established, and at this time the apparently unlimited space left little reason to contemplate higher density.

Zoning depicted in Bartholomew's 1946 map supported a vision of West Vancouver as a semi-urban development where waterfront lots of modest size gave way to larger lots as one moved farther away from the water and up the mountain. Most of Ambleside and Dundarave were designated for smaller lot sizes of 6,000 square feet (about seven units per acre), as well as the reserve area west of the Capilano River (although not likely with the Indigenous residents in mind). A smaller area along the Ambleside waterfront and in Dundarave between 23rd and 25th was set aside for semi-detached two-family homes, which were permitted no more than four boarders or lodgers. The waterfront from Dundarave west to Cypress Park was allocated lot sizes of 9,000 square feet (about five units per acre). The largest portion (6,513 acres) was set aside for lot sizes of 12,000 square feet (about 3.5 units per acre) with 80-foot (24-metre) frontages. This included the initial development of the British Properties and the Capilano Reserve east of Capilano River. A chunk of 1,200 acres was designated for "country homes" with lots of at least two acres and a minimum frontage of 200 feet (60 metres). This area was in the northern portion of West Vancouver, above the British Properties, which at this time had no streets and almost no development. A good portion of this is above the 1,200-foot (364-metre) level, although no houses appear to have been built there. Frontages for all residences were generous, with at least 75 to 80 feet (about 24 metres) required in all except the older sections. Even here, frontages of at least 50 feet (15 metres) were recommended; 33 feet (10 metres) was considered too small. Many of their recommendations were incorporated into Bylaw 1188, passed in 1947.

The 1,200-foot (364-metre) limit on development in West Vancouver became a guideline in the '50s, originally because that was the limit to which water services could be provided. Improved technology makes service to higher areas possible (if expensive), but that limit has been retained in the interests of protecting the fragile environment at higher levels. This has given West Vancouver, when viewed from the Lions Gate Bridge, a more or less straight line across its northern boundary of development, unlike the District of North Vancouver, the limits of whose development are adapted to the terrain. From time to time suggestions have been made to limit development on more rugged terrain at lower levels in return for development of land higher up, but so far the 1,200-foot level has remained sacrosanct. The Hollyburn cabins, at a higher level, are an exception, but these use no municipal services.

Bartholomew generally dismissed apartments from his plans. "The fact that but two or three apartment houses have been erected in West Vancouver is conclusive proof that this type of residence has not been needed," he noted in one of his reports, which further considered the "blighting effect on the surrounding single-family homes." It appears that the assumption was that these would be rentals. Those who lived in and owned their own residences were preferred members of the community, as they were perceived as more stable, long-term residents. The concept and legal structure for owner-occupied apartments was in any case not generally in place at this time.

Bartholomew's plans to keep West Vancouver a community of single-family homes were soon overtaken by other developments. The reality of tax revenue needed for the expensive infrastructure of a growing industry-free city became hard to ignore. Baynes's arguments and Pidgeon's actions were a conservative rearguard action against the fear of unchecked growth, whether it was in the form of commercial enterprise or apartment buildings. They did not foresee that in the future more revenue would be needed if taxation were not to rise to a level that the average West Vancouver homeowner would find intolerable. Two possible avenues for augmented taxation presented themselves: industry and apartments.

> Ourselves and our neighbours are surprised at the high taxes we are about to pay this year. In several cases we had friends now living in Vancouver who looked forward to the time when they might have a house in West Vancouver with a decent lot size and where the taxes would be reasonable. I am rather afraid that these people will now realize that it is more economical to live in Vancouver.[12]
>
> —Ted Baynes

Some believed that, with over 90 per cent of tax revenue coming from private property, light industry was the most secure path to increase revenue. Taxes on light industry were possibly more stable than those from private residences, and had the advantage of making little or no call for the funding of schools or other services. Perhaps memories of the multitudes of tax sales of private property and the near bankruptcy of the municipality a few years earlier were still fresh in people's minds. This view received little support, as most West Vancouverites have traditionally opposed opening the door to new industry.

Renowned urban planner Peter Oberlander's 1954 report confirmed the difficulty of generating revenue in a non-industrial single-family community. "Land sub-division at a high single-family detached home standard usually does not pay for the range and quality of municipal services expected by most suburban families....the key to West Vancouver's wider tax base, and therefore, more secure income, lies in diversification." He believed communities needed to reflect "the closely interwoven pattern of daily life" with housing, shopping, recreation and schools integrated with each other. Housing types needed to reflect West Vancouver's increasing demographic diversity, where older residents and childless couples were becoming more numerous. Unfortunately, this happened only in a very limited way. West Vancouver development has always been playing catch-up with its demographics.

In 1951, then reeve Howard Fletcher realized that some change of direction was needed to augment tax revenue, and went so far as to hold informal talks with Vancouver politicians about amalgamating the two cities. This did not sit well with his fellow townsmen, who sought other solutions, particularly building apartments. Fletcher then asked council to rezone a block for apartment purposes on the south side of Haywood between 24th and 25th, and by 1959 six apartment buildings consisting of 115 suites had been constructed east of 24th and south of Marine, where now stands the Seastrand. Mr. and Mrs. E. Willard Graham had built the Mariner Apartments on 19th Street in 1954. A number of other plans for apartments did not materialize. In 1952, plans to replace the Great Northern Cannery with a shopping centre and apartments, and in 1954 to build apartments for the north side of Sentinel Hill, were both non-starters.

A tenuous consensus was finally reached that apartments provided a logical, perhaps inevitable, way of accommodating West Vancouver's diverse and growing population, while also providing a base for increased tax revenue. Original plans called for an area of one hundred acres for new apartments. This was abbreviated in 1959 to fifty acres in the Ambleside area, with the height of buildings limited to twenty storeys. These occupied much of the old tent and shack area from between 18th and 22nd, mostly on or near the waterfront on Argyle and Bellevue Streets. This permanently changed West Vancouver, to the dismay of many who lamented the wall of concrete towers that erupted on the waterfront, often blocking their stunning views.

Crescent Apartments, designed by Kevin Gardner and Warnett Kennedy and opened in 1961, was the first apartment building in this plan. The apartment zoning bylaw was not completed until the apartment was well advanced, so each influenced the other. The apartment was curved, as its name suggests, to fit the site and maximize the panoramic view, featuring large outdoor balconies, a swimming pool and a shared roof garden. Although the apartments in this building were self-owned, those in a number of ensuing buildings were rentals.

A little farther east, not far from Harvey Haddon's ill-fated mansion in the woods, the garden apartments of Spuraway heralded new concepts in urban living. Originally purchased by Edward Mahon in 1910, from 1923 the land was developed by George Herrmann into a farm and equestrian centre. The original log house, built in 1911 and still standing, became the core of the spacious home, Spuraway. In 1953, Gordon Gibson, Sr. and his wife, Louise, bought Lot 3 and continued the development of a convivial community, much in the spirit of recent developments in co-housing. The International Land Corporation (ILC) purchased this land in 1965 and built a number of townhouses with spacious grounds and acres of gardens, to which they added a six-storey apartment building in 1968. The log house, with extensive additions, remains a sumptuous private club for residents.

By 1964, 35 apartment buildings were either completed or under construction in Ambleside, many echoing Miami Beach's apartment hotels. Between 1961 and 1971, 1,800 new detached homes and 3,100 apartment units led to West Vancouver's rapid growth from 25,500 to 36,500, and to an increase in tax revenue amounting to 13–14 per cent of the municipal budget. The need for the new apartments was clear from the 1 per cent rental vacancy rate in 1975, although few rentals have been built since to satisfy that need and current vacancy rates are generally well below 1 per cent. In 1974, Daon proposed developing up to two thousand units of low-rental housing, but no suitable municipal land was deemed available.

In spite of the need for apartments, development proposals often fomented conflict between developers and local citizens' groups. Residents often argued that council should not allow developers to block their view, cause congested traffic and pose hazards for emergency vehicles. But once the rules for development in the apartment zone were laid down, construction that observed these rules could not legally be refused.

Major provocation came when, in 1967, Bill Irwin and Associates formulated a plan to reclaim eighty acres of the waterfront between 19th and 23rd, stretching up to five hundred metres from the natural shoreline, on which they would build twenty-five buildings as high as forty storeys and containing six thousand suites. This development would include three public beaches, swimming pools, tennis courts, pitch-and-putt golf courses and a shopping centre.

Public outcry led council to nix this plan, so the developers came

By 1984, West Van's coastline was dominated by clusters of apartment buildings. At 14th Street, the prime waterfront itself was occupied by a decaying Ferry Building, flanked by a bus depot and repair shop. *West Vancouver Museum and Archives, 2500.0038.DWV*

back with a smaller project, called Laguna del Mar, at the foot of 22nd, which would include a still extensive six banks of five-storey townhouses and a twenty-six-storey tower with a total of four hundred units. The developer, Jack Poole, proposed this be built on an artificial peninsula at Navvy Jack Point. This was defeated by council in the spring of 1969.[13]

These threats to the integrity of West Vancouver's magnificent waterfront led a group of citizens to organize The West Vancouver Preservation Society. This developed into the Citizens' Planning Forum, a group of about thirty people, which was incorporated under the Societies Act on September 23, 1969. "The goal was tasteful development blending with the natural environment."[14] This group, along with ratepayer groups from the different communities, did much to shape and direct the municipal dialogue over the next decades. Generally, they have been successful in preserving West Vancouver's remarkable beauty and limiting its population, but the success of the latter has been a partial cause of the extraordinary increase in housing costs. Generally ratepayers' groups have opposed changes that would increase density. Zoning or the denial of services have been used as ways to control growth.

In the early '70s, many considered population growth West Vancouver's biggest problem. From a 1971 population of 36,500, it grew to 39,000 by 1975. At this rate, residents feared growth to over 60,000 by the turn of the century. In reality, the population in 2017 was just over 42,000 and declining. In 1975 Mayor Jones named then councillor Rod Day to chair a task force on growth in West Vancouver. This committee concluded that low-cost housing in West Vancouver is not possible, and noted that efforts must concentrate on attracting young professional families to live there. Day saw the danger of West Vancouver growing "in a demographically and socially unbalanced manner, and that, by the 1980s, this could result in an over-aged and very affluent community increasingly isolated from other communities in the Lower Mainland."[15]

One of the major battles occurred over development plans for the southeast corner of Taylor Way and Marine Drive. Much of this prime real estate at West Vancouver's eastern gateway had been acquired in the 1930s through tax sales. In 1981 the municipality purchased additional land for $1 million that had been used by the General Motors dealership. The municipality zoned it for high-rise development, proposing two twenty-one-storey residential towers, with future BPP Manager Jim McLean managing the negotiations. The municipality wanted the revenue that leasing the land would provide, although many residents preferred a park.

Vigorous objections from citizens' groups initially prevented plans from proceeding. In 1986, the city again explored residential use of the land, with many residents continuing to express opposition to plans for the two high-rises. The land was leased to Newcorp Properties and the municipal government threw all its resources into supporting its building plans, which a 1988 referendum narrowly rejected 5,872 to 5,830. The municipality decided to go ahead anyway and the apartments were built.

Many of those who favoured the apartments now feel vindicated. Revenue to the municipality from the ninety-nine-year lease of land has been put into an endowment fund to finance many of West Vancouver's

Small businesses—corner grocery stores and gas stations—were dotted along Marine Drive for several decades. The Ridge Store and Wetmore Motors anchored the corner of 22nd and Marine Drive for decades, the Ridge being a favourite after-school haunt for kids from Pauline Johnson School just up the street. Most of these family businesses are gone now, replaced by larger, more sophisticated developments.
West Vancouver Memorial Library, 1435.WVML

subsequent public projects, especially the community centres. It also provided $4 million toward the purchase of the Wetmore Motors site in 2003 at 2203 Marine Drive (total cost: $5.5 million), which has now become a large complex of mixed commercial/residential (apartments). Leveraging development to bankroll future projects has since become a common policy.

This struggle raised other questions. If a proposal meets all zoning and design criteria, but is opposed by a majority of the community, should it be allowed? Successive councils have wrestled with this thorny issue, but have generally resisted the downzoning of multi-unit areas to single-family use, which many citizens' groups have urged. In 1980, downzoning for nine sites in the Ambleside area was rejected, and in 1981 council also defeated a proposal to downzone fourteen waterfront apartment sites

Once the site of the Ridge Store and Wetmore Motors, the corner of 22nd and Marine is now home to a small café and seniors' residences. Times have changed. *Photo by John Moir*

from high-rise to low-rise. Don Lanskail, mayor of West Vancouver from 1986 to 1990, voiced strong opposition to downzoning, considering it to be "morally wrong and unfair to destroy substantial property values by arbitrarily changing rules that had existed for 23 years." By 1974, the municipality was actively discouraging detached single-family dwellings in some areas, considering it a poor use of land. Others felt that, in spite of the tax revenue generated, the original decision to zone this area for apartments was a mistake, fearing that West Vancouver would become another West End, with increased crime and other urban problems some thought were associated with high density.

The rapid apartment-fuelled growth of the '60s led to visions of still greater development. The report with the lengthy if accurate name "Draft Report for the Working Committee on Potential Urban Development on Slopes and Elevations Above the 1200 ft. Contour and Over," dated July 9, 1973, took an unusually flexible approach to development up the mountain. It proposed that land above the 1,200-foot (364-metre) level on the North Shore could provide living space for 20,000 people in the following ten years, and eventually 30,000. While in favour of major population increases, it recognized that the natural features warranted preservation, the watershed needed protection and there was no public appetite for developing Cypress Bowl or Hollyburn Ridge. These grandiose plans did not get beyond the drawing board.

The 1974 Advisory Commission on the Upper Levels proposed similar if more modest plans. They recommended a centrally located satellite hospital in West Vancouver for non-acute care, as well as neighbourhood stores and gas stations, and discouraged single-family residences. Again, these plans generally did not materialize.

The more radical developments and proposals in the early '70s generated a strong conservative reaction to change from many residents later that decade. The West Vancouver Residents for Controlled Growth proclaimed that "the unique quality of life in West Vancouver, as compared with other cities, is primarily dependent on low density." Its opposition to development paralleled the American anti-growth tax-revolt movements in the '70s, inspired by the affluent inhabitants of the Marin Bay area of San Francisco. In 1976, the residents' group urged West Vancouverites to "bestir themselves to exert political pressure to ensure slow and orderly growth in this little part of God's green acre." There were only seventy-nine housing starts in that year. Even visitors, many of them passing through on their way to Whistler, were at times discouraged from stopping. The 1978 West Vancouver Planning Commission stated that "tourists should not be encouraged to visit West Vancouver nor should park or waterfront facilities particularly be advertised for non-municipal resident use."

Some remained secure in the belief that now was forever. The 1980 Official Community Plan (OCP) reflected the mood of many citizens, proposing "to preserve what we have, an era of control and fine tuning." But standing still is not an option in today's world. While fear of uncontrolled growth was and is a legitimate concern, problems of escalating house prices caused by low or no growth remained largely unaddressed. Assumptions that younger families would replace aging families were derailed by housing costs that placed purchases far beyond the reach of the average family. The number of seniors continued to grow. The population declined between 1976 and 1981.

In a detailed and prescient article in the *North and West Voice*,[16] Mike Steele unpacked the implications of the no-growth position. Vancouver councillor Gordon Price said that many on the North Shore "simply don't want change but [they] expect the rest of the region to bear the consequences." No-growth policies, he said, pose "a very severe danger… in terms of accommodating change, of providing for people at different stages of their lives, at different incomes, at different ages." This would lead to "a net loss of population. The children can't afford to live there, they move out." This has been borne out in the years since.

Increased density has been a tough sell. A 1986 survey indicated that 94 per cent of respondents wanted to either maintain or reduce the density as defined in the 1980 OCP. Some feared population increases in West Vancouver to as much as 70,000, and even the Residents for Controlled Growth predicted an increase to 49,314 based on 1980 zoning.

Attendees at a public meeting to the OCP's 1988 update "showed great resistance to change . . . they were especially unhappy with the prospect of further encroachment of higher density residential development."[17] Density has remained much less than in most other Lower Mainland communities, with a limit of from 0.5 to 2.5 units per acre in the Upper Lands. In older neighbourhoods, including the apartment area, densities have crept higher, ranging from four to more than twenty-five units per acre. Panorama Village has a density of sixteen units per acre. New developments are often allowed higher density.

Privately, some were more receptive to change. Correspondence to the municipal hall in the 1980s often supported greater density and cluster housing. Many expressed particular concern that the dearth of younger families and the increase in older residents would "affect taxation and business growth: seniors tend to spend less while requiring more tax-funded services. The only solution is increased densities to provide more affordable housing for younger families and even a proportion of seniors themselves."[18] Many feared greater density would lead to greater crime, but as the experience of Vancouver's West End and many other urban communities bears out, there is little or no connection between the two. Don Lanskail, like most successive mayors, left the door to growth at least a little ajar, considering that we "have to accept our modest share of growth while maintaining and enhancing our quality of life."

The combination of smaller families, an aging population and the growth of private schools has inevitably led to a decline in the public school population. Enrolment reached a peak of 8,679 in 1969, but then declined steadily to 4,869 in 1986. From 1979 to 2001, the projected decline in West Vancouver was the highest of any BC school district. Total enrolment now ranges between seven and eight thousand, but this includes substantial numbers from outside the catchment area, and foreign students. So far all schools have remained open.

West Vancouver's population has declined in two recent periods: from 1976 to 1981 and from 2011 to 2016. In both cases, high house prices were major factors, although it is troubling that the more recent decline took place during a period of strong economic growth. The high prices mean that many who work here live elsewhere, with the community becoming increasingly composed of older people who bought property when it was more affordable and recent arrivals who have deep pockets but often a tenuous connection to the community.

The matter of West Vancouver's population and its widely discussed recent decline needs some clarification. The BC Stats figures that came out in early 2017 reported a decrease of population from 42,923 in 2011 to 40,923 in 2016. That significant drop—of 2,000 people or 4.7 per cent of the population—initiated a bout of soul searching. But when the Canadian census figures came out later in the year, they showed a much more modest decline from 42,694 to 42,473, or 0.5 per cent, for the same period. The difference, apparently, lies mainly in the method of obtaining data, and Canadian census figures are considered more reliable. In any case, West Vancouver is not about to become a ghost town and much of the discrepancy between the two figures is explainable by other circumstances, such as the large number of West Vancouverites who live here for only part of the year and may or may not be counted as resident. Still, it does raise some interesting questions about the use of statistics. A difference of 1,550 in a small city is a big difference.

A Game of Homes

The houses of the 1940s, '50s and '60s were generally built to merge into the landscape, with the house having a relatively small footprint and landscaping enhancing its appearance and livability. Lots were relatively spacious, some arguing this was needed because early houses used septic fields rather than being on sewage systems. This changed in the 1970s and '80s when many houses maximized their footprint on the lot, standing out as ostentatious displays, with lots often shorn of natural vegetation. One resident used his yard to throw a christening party for his twelve-metre yacht, which he had moored in his swimming pool.

Huge houses are not a recent phenomenon, as anyone who has driven through Shaughnessy will be well aware. In the early years of this past century, immense wealth fuelled the building of many mansions. Structures such as the present University Women's Club, whose ballroom in its days as a private residence could accommodate two hundred guests, were once private homes; the ten-acre Shannon estate at Granville and 57th, once home to sugar king Benjamin Rogers, now accommodates several hundred guests in the original home and numerous infill developments.

The current concern with large houses dates from the 1970s. In 1974, motivated by a desire to increase the availability of building lots during an escalating real estate market, New Westminster became the first Lower Mainland community to take action. The problem was even more central to West Vancouver with its emphasis on upscale single-family homes. From around 1980, the municipality responded to widespread community dissatisfaction with the growing number of large houses, many of which changed the physical character of traditional neighbourhoods.

Since then, gaining control of the size and nature of houses being built has been one of the main challenges for the municipality of West Vancouver. In 1980, council introduced floor-area ratio regulations to control the amount of floor space permitted in new homes, with more restrictive height regulations following.[19] Former director of planning Steve Nicholls noted that zoning could control anything that can be measured, such as fences, hedges and size of houses. It cannot (under current bylaws) control the appearance of single-family homes, although it can in multi-family dwellings.

Planning and development consultant Donald Barcham noted in his 1988 report "The Large House Syndrome" that, while the municipality tacitly recognized that much of the new development, particularly single-family homes, was an aesthetic and environmental disaster, it also benefited from the increased taxes that larger homes (and apartment developments) brought in. Tax revenues can double when large houses replace modest ones. In a community with a largely residential tax base, that's a major practical consideration. Taxes pay for infrastructure such as roads, plumbing and sewage, which are extremely expensive on the rocky terrain of the North Shore.

Barcham noted that although height regulations were introduced in 1984, "Most new homes are built on platforms cut into the hillside with little regard for slope, tree cover, or natural features." This makes the height of a building difficult to define and limit. He commented that:

> *The challenge before Council and the community is to decide whether to resist the market trends and severely restrict house size in an attempt to preserve neighbourhood character, existing views and the parklike setting, or to continue to accommodate the apparent market, but devise ways of integrating larger new homes into the established aesthetics of our community.*[20]

Council has generally favoured the latter position. Whether or not council intended it, the trend to large houses has continued. Many owners, who may have paid several million dollars for their property, have argued for the freedom to build what they liked and often found ways to circumvent or ignore municipal rules. Some critics of this trend have felt West Vancouver, particularly the British Properties, was "mutating into stuccoed wastelands where simple family homes resemble mid-sized apartment blocks." Or as architect Arthur Erickson commented simply in 1997, "appalling."

Council passed a bylaw in 1989 restricting house size by regulating site coverage, deleting building-depth regulations, restricting paved surfaces to 50 per cent of the yard and limiting the height of walls, such as retaining walls along streets necessitated by the steep mountain slopes. Enforcement of a blasting bylaw has at times required builders to restore rock they've blasted. As Nicholls mentioned, the problem with bylaws is that they are written for the 5 per cent of people who abuse them, but he is pleased that those implemented in the '80s were among the most restrictive in Greater Vancouver.

The arrival of Asian money has often been blamed for huge houses, but many were built in the 1960s, long before the influx of wealthy Asian immigrants. That notwithstanding, it is true that the success of Expo 86 was a watershed moment in Lower Mainland development, as Vancouver launched itself onto the world stage, becoming a major destination for Hong Kong citizens fearing the results of their community's return to China in 1997. Many houses built at this time show little consideration for the surrounding architectural or natural environment, a major change from the modernist principles that informed the best architecture of an earlier generation. Councillor Rod Day expressed particular concern

Problems of outsized houses have continued to vex neighbourhoods well into the 2000s. New houses weighing in at over 12,000 square feet leave the neighbours feeling overwhelmed. *Photo by Ian Smith*

with the "environmental disasters" that were, in the 1980s and '90s, destroying the landscape. His frustration was palpable: "The problem is that it has been hard to get the bylaws written soon enough before some developer finds some new and ingenious way to get around them." In 1996, he sponsored a new bylaw that required reduction of the permitted building footprint, more space between buildings, a minimum of three metres setback from creeks and no more than three garage doors facing the street.

When Hong Kong was returned to Chinese control in 1997, the press reported that some local houses were being built with karaoke rooms and Chinese-style kitchens. In its privileged position on the Pacific Rim, the Vancouver area has become a Shangri-la for many Asians; West Vancouver has particular appeal in providing space and privacy hard to find in the average Asian city. Recent popular Chinese films often evoke Vancouver as an ideal place to escape to.

In the past thirty years, West Vancouver's record in creating housing that reflects community demographics, values and aspirations has at best been mixed. Most of the houses built in the past decade, generally as replacements for older houses, are around 6,000 to 7,000 square feet, although a number sprawl to upwards of 10,000 square feet. Most sell on the upside of $5 million. Even modest homes top $3 million, nearly all of which is the lot price. Few younger families (or older ones for that matter) can afford these prices.

Municipal policy that maintains relatively low density while allowing the building of large houses increases the human footprint. In *The New Urban Crisis*, Richard Florida cites a UCLA study of wealthy Malibu, California, where the density is about one person per acre but energy use per capita is more than ten times that in the working class suburb of Bell, with about twenty-two persons per acre.[21] Delivery costs of water and energy are also higher in more dispersed areas. All other things being equal, low density places a greater stress on the environment.

An over-heated real estate market has recent buyers elbowing their way alongside more traditional homes to take advantage of the best waterfront views.
Photo by John Moir

High house prices have been a fact of life for a long time in West Vancouver. ". . . if I sign this mortgage at these prices it won't be the land of the free but it sure will be the home of the brave," was the caption for this Len Norris cartoon of 1967. Norris was very aware of West Van house prices: he lived there. See page 189.
West Vancouver Museum and Archives, 008.WVA.NOR

A house built beginning in 2016 in the 1700 block of Mathers Avenue sprawls to an astonishing 26,000 square feet, making it drastically out of character with the relatively modest surrounding homes. It includes an indoor/outdoor pool, badminton court, movie theatre and virtual golf room. Technically it breaks no municipal rules. According to current regulations, 35 per cent of the lot's surface area is buildable, but the basement does not count in the square footage. The property's owner assembled two lots totalling 48,954 square feet on which a two-level house plus a basement could be built on the 35 per cent allowable (17,134 square feet). Two levels makes for an allowable 34,268 square feet, so the house is well within municipal parameters.

Even though a bylaw has been passed with the goal of preventing the construction of future houses of this scale, a number of householders used this loophole to combine adjacent lots and initiate similar developments before the bylaw was passed. Future houses in Ambleside are now limited to a paltry 6,300 square feet, although property owners can apply for a variance to build larger homes. How large a home should be allowed? As former municipal planner Steve Nicholls said, each neighbourhood has a character, but it's difficult to articulate, and encapsulating it in a bylaw is nigh impossible.

Modest cottages have often become multimillion-dollar residences. A waterfront cottage at 3666 Marine Drive, built by the redoubtable Captain Summersgill Snoddy, was originally valued at $3,080. Purchased by Phil and Pat Boname in 1970 for $190,000, it was expanded to about 4,000 square feet and sold for $7.8 million in 2009 as a tear-down. A new house built on this site in 2014 was assessed at $7,517,000 in 2017. That's an increase of almost 2,500 times the original cost.

Numerous Shades of Grey

West Vancouver is home to large numbers of older people. In the 2016 census, 11,810 people or 27.8 per cent of the population was over sixty-five. This compares with 15.7 per cent of the population of Greater Vancouver, and is a small but significant increase from 25.5 per cent in the 2011 census for West Vancouver. Although the community is largely tailored to their needs, it's not all it might be. The 2017 Vital Signs report from the West Vancouver Community Foundation states that West Vancouver's low walkability score (43 out of a scale of 100) and low transit accessibility increases social isolation and has negative effects on health and well-being, especially for older people. Many cannot afford the single-family homes in West Vancouver, which have until recently been its main housing option. But many also cannot afford to live in the upscale seniors' residences that have been built in recent years.

A few seniors' residences built in the 1970s, such as Libby Lodge, Capilano Towers and Kiwanis Village, provided relatively low-cost accommodation. Libby Lodge in Horseshoe Bay contains eight one-bedroom apartments of 450 square feet, and thirty-seven studios at 360–420 square feet. In ensuing years, the need for places for seniors grew. In 1982, the West Vancouver Seniors Housing Committee, formed to project how many seniors would need housing by 1992, recommended 133 units of nonprofit housing, with 245 additional intermediate care beds. The Klahanee Park Lodge, a joint venture of the North Shore Rotary clubs and CMHC, opened in 1992 with 105 units.

Progress has recently been made in meeting seniors' needs for reasonable accommodation, although the trend in the last thirty years has been toward market-driven homes, often for an affluent clientele. Generally the units are much larger than in earlier buildings, mostly composed of one- or two-bedroom apartments rather than studios. Hollyburn House, West Vancouver's first private retirement home, which opened in 1986, includes a bar, hair salon, whirlpool and private meeting rooms. Its success (the waiting list is about one year) has provided impetus for similar developments, including Amica, the Westerleigh and La Maison, all geared toward middle- and upper-income residents. This is largely driven by West Vancouver's booming real estate market, which provides a tidy nest egg for many home-owning, downsizing seniors. Those who did not own homes may not be so lucky.

Seniors who can no longer afford accommodation in their community must look for residences up the Fraser Valley, on the Sunshine Coast or on Vancouver Island, often leaving behind family, friends and neighbourhood services. In 2012, only 274 social housing units existed for seniors, although some assisted housing has become available in new developments. In that year, 51 per cent of West Vancouver seniors earned less than $30,000 a year.

Age Matters

With aging people, so with aging homes. How to protect West Vancouver's heritage from the pressures of development? In 1979, the North Shore Heritage Advisory Committee was formed to complete an inventory of North Shore structures, with committees subsequently established for each of the three North Shore communities. The West Vancouver Heritage Inventory was completed in 1988.

For a site to be designated as "heritage," which means it cannot be altered or demolished, the municipality must own it. Currently only five locations in West Vancouver are so designated. These are the Ferry Building, the Gertrude Lawson House and three private residences: the Binning House at 2968 Mathers Crescent, designed in 1941 by artist Bertram Charles Binning; the Wagner residence at 6003 Eagleridge Drive, designed in 1963 by Percy Underwood; and the Toby House at 2055 Queens, designed in 1962 by Ray Toby. If a building is on the community heritage register but not owned by the city, demolition can be delayed for sixty days while the owners consider options that may encourage them to save their house. The municipality can sometimes negotiate a deal with the developer. In other cases, a heritage structure can be incorporated into a new development, thus satisfying (to some extent) both economic and aesthetic considerations.

In 1996, Lower Caulfeild was designated a conservation area under BC's Municipal Act to conserve its heritage value and character-defining elements. This community of narrow winding streets, verdant landscapes and spectacular views remains one of the most distinctive in the Lower Mainland, retaining much of the charm fostered by Francis Caulfeild, with St. Francis-in-the-Woods Church providing both a spiritual and social focus. New houses or significant alterations to Caulfeild homes must first be approved by the municipality's planning department and then by the Lower Caulfeild Advisory Committee. The vegetation and the natural slopes of the land must be retained.

But the ambience is under continual threat. Whereas some Caulfeild residents want to respect the heritage character of their properties, others prefer maximizing their investment. Many local owners and builders, who were vocal in their objection to new large houses and the incompatible design of some, backed off when they realized that enforcing regulations on the size and nature of new homes would have a negative effect on the value of their own properties, as any purchasers of their property would in turn have their options and potential profit limited. The trend in the last ten years has been to building to the maximum allowable square footage on the lot, resulting in some huge houses that are incompatible with the neighbourhood. Some builders have blithely ignored stop-work permits and cut down trees, contrary to municipal policy. Some local residents feel that both the committee and municipal staff could at times be tougher at enforcing the rules. Developers are often adept at manipulating the guidelines to their advantage—or simply ignoring them.

Dianne Sherwood, a voice for the Caulfeild that was, inhabits a heritage home with a stunning view of Pilot Cove built by Captain Frank Kettle, who at one point sailed on that most renowned of the old clippers, the Cutty Sark. Sherwood fears that, as older Caulfeild homes are demolished, their replacements often do not respect the natural diversity of the landscape, as Francis Caulfeild would have wished. She feels that, while Caulfeild's original community allowed for lots of varying sizes and shapes, current developers often eliminate the inconsistencies of the land in their construction, making the land fit the house rather than the reverse. The community, she believes, would thrive on more inconsistency, and being "wild, natural and crazy." Smaller houses adapted to the land is her wish.

As the value of houses has escalated, new residents are shaping Caulfeild with their elaborate homes while others are fighting hard to preserve its integrity. The struggle by those close to its heart continues. How can individual freedom be balanced with community needs? And who is the community? With so many diverse individuals and such complex community needs as West Vancouver grows and changes, the answer to this question slowly evolves.

From his room on West Georgia, views of the snow-capped mountains intrigued him. On the Norwegian holiday of May 17, 1922, [Rudolph] Verne set off with a friend to explore potential ski country on the North Shore. Their intended destination was Grouse Mountain, but boarding the wrong ferry landed them in West Vancouver.

—Francis Mansbridge, *Hollyburn: The Mountain and the City*, p. 34

Seen in the upper right of this 1916/17 photo, flumes carried shingle bolts through the wild Capilano Canyon to small mills in West Vancouver.
West Vancouver Museum and Archives, Leonard Frank photo, 008.WVA.JOH

02

COMMUNITIES TAKING SHAPE/CHANGING SHAPE

Logging the Slopes

Before European settlers arrived, coastal Indigenous people inhabited a primeval forest that nourished their needs. Huge trees, up to three metres or more in diameter, especially western red cedar, provided material for baskets and clothing, and tools for household and other needs. The new settlers also found that these trees satisfied many needs, making shingles, shakes and all kinds of furniture for homes throughout North America and beyond. To extract the timber, the early logging companies built ingenious combinations of roads, railways and flumes; some succeeded while others were glorious and expensive failures. Flumes transported cedar shingle bolts from the mountains to the mills, also doubling as routes on which young adventurers took perilous but exciting rides. These, along with railways and skid roads, later provided some of the routes for the first streets where early settlers built their homes.

Like Rudolph Verne (see epigraph on opposite page), many looked to the North Shore as a place where dreams could become reality. A few years earlier, Sewell Moody had set up his logging business, the Moodyville Sawmill Company, in North Vancouver. The first operator on the scene, in 1870 he obtained two logging leases in what is now West Vancouver. Attempts to log the lease at the mouth of Cypress Creek proved unsuccessful. The more productive lease, much of which became the British Properties, stretched west from the Capilano River to the current 22nd Street, and back nearly eight kilometres from the water, although Moody did not log most of it. He set up his logging camp on the present Ambleside Beach, using seven yoke of oxen to haul the logs to his mill. This camp operated until about 1890, with the last of the skid roads in the British Properties not disappearing until about 1934.

A number of mills operated in West Vancouver in the early twentieth century, primarily attracted by the cedar—the Indigenous people's tree of life became the tree of economic returns for the early pioneers, although hopes of high profits were often dashed on the difficulties of felling and moving the huge trees. From 1906 the McNair Timber Company operated on Moody's old lease, building a log dump at the foot of 16th Street and constructing a railway to transport cedar from terrain that was too steep for the oxen to navigate. These logs were used primarily to create shingle bolts, and from these, shingles. In 1908 they brought in the Walking Dudley, supposedly named after a logger who walked from camp to camp. The first of its kind in BC, this 38-ton machine pulled itself along on a grip wheel that engaged cables on each side of the rails. With the logs debarked on one side to slide better along the greased track, this machine could move up to twenty logs at one time. Berry pickers sometimes hitched free rides on the little flat cars attached to its downhill end. Fortunately, none were riding when the Dudley slipped its brakes and careened down the mountain slope, tipping front first into the inlet when it reached the end of the wharf.

One of the largest operators was the Capilano Timber Company, established in 1917. Capilano built a flume that clung perilously to the sides of Capilano Canyon, transporting shingle bolts; some sources indicate it also carried approximately five-metre link bolts, which were used for lumber panelling. A later logging railway transported logs on railcars down the Capilano River Valley from deep in the wilderness, well past the Lions mountains. The company ceased operations when the mill at the foot of Pemberton Avenue in North Vancouver burned in 1932.

From 1928, several independent horse loggers worked the upper slopes. G.G. Johnson cleared the Glenmore area northeast of the new British Properties development and worked west to Horseshoe Bay, clear-cutting the area from the 500-foot (150-metre) level to 1,200 feet

(364 metres). Apart from a few locations such as Lighthouse Park, little old-growth now remains on the North Shore.

Early logging was selective, although the motivation had less to do with environmental sensitivity than a desire to select the best and most easily accessible timber. With increased mechanization in the 1920s, clear-cutting became the norm, laying large areas to waste with little regard for protecting creeks or rehabilitating the devastated landscape. Logging companies left behind roads and cleared land that later opened up space for new development, but they also left mounds of debris, which posed a major fire hazard. Slash fires burn at temperatures up to 1,814° Fahrenheit, destroying much of the organic layer in the soil and leading to severe erosion. Mostly the forest was left to regenerate itself or slowly be transformed into streets where settlers built their dream homes.

By 1913, a community was forming around the ferry dock at the foot of 14th Street. The gently sloping cleared landscape in the area made possible a relatively orderly grid pattern of streets. The Pacific Great Eastern Railway was constructing a stop just behind the Ferry Building, shifting the commercial and transportation focus of the community away from John Lawson's more westerly acreage. *West Vancouver Museum and Archives, 0342.WVA.RAH*

Early Land Acquisition and Development

By 1890, plans for the new town of Newcastle on the North Shore, inspired by the English coal port of that name, were well underway. "Lots will be offered by the Burrard Inlet Coal Syndicate this morning at the office of Ross, Ceperly and Tatlow-Spinks. The vein of coal existing there is thought to be part of the Nanaimo formation."[22] Fortunately, the promoters' plans were premature; the supply and quality of coal were insufficient to justify riddling the North Shore with coal mines, and it was some time before development became a reality. But this did lead to the 1891 incorporation of the District of North Vancouver, stretching across the whole North Shore from Deep Cove to Horseshoe Bay.

In 1907, the McNair–Fraser Logging Company built a rail line to move logs extending from the foot of 16th Street to an upper camp, pictured here, at about the site of the highest house in the British Properties. To manage the steep grades of up to 16 per cent, the hapless Walking Dudley (seen on the right) was employed. By 1914 the tree resource had been exhausted, the rails taken up and Hollyburn Ridge was a less than pretty sight. *City of Vancouver Archives, AM54-S4-: Log P50.1*

Little is known about Navvy Jack Thomas, the first non-Indigenous year-round resident in West Vancouver. He had jumped ship about 1866, forty years before the next settlers. He began what we might now refer to as an "über" ferry service between the North Shore and the mainland for the sporadic visitors, and made his reputation and income extracting sand and gravel from the west side of the Capilano River, known at the time as Navvy Jack gravel for its high quality. His house, originally located at 17th and Bellevue, was moved a half block west to what is now 1768 Argyle. Built about 1873, it is still standing, the longest continually occupied house in the Lower Mainland, acquired in 1996 by the municipality.

One of the District of North Vancouver's first acts was to begin building Keith Road as the east-west communication route from Deep Cove to Horseshoe Bay. This predated the initial development of West Vancouver by at least fifteen years, and while lack of use and an economic depression in the 1890s led to the road becoming overgrown west of the Capilano River, it did eventually open up many areas of West Vancouver to access. Its West Vancouver section mostly followed the route of the present Marine Drive. Other roads were rough; Inglewood was a loose road with broken planks guaranteed to strike you if you stepped on the wrong end. The large rocks on 13th Street made it difficult to navigate, even for walkers.

Assorted land speculators and eccentrics drifted in and out of West Vancouver in the late nineteenth century, but no one stayed long; major development did not commence until early in the next century. Most communities had one major developer who bought up a large chunk of land. Most were (or became) wealthy, and many were well educated, traits that have become synonymous with West Vancouver ever since. The most important of these were John Lawson, Francis Caulfeild and Edward Mahon.

John Lawson arrived in Vancouver in 1905, but looked north across Burrard Inlet for new frontiers. When he rowed across the inlet with his brother-in-law Alexander Smith on April 23, 1907, strong tidal currents swept them past the mouth of the Capilano River to what would become Ambleside (then Hollyburn). Lawson acquired all the properties between what are now 16th and 18th Streets from the waterfront to Haywood, as well as eleven acres on 20th Street between the waterfront and Haywood. His land included what had been Navvy Jack's house, where he lived from 1907 to 1928.

With his family, including his brother-in-law William Thompson, Lawson developed the community that became the core of West Vancouver. He brought in phone service, headquartered in the West Vancouver Stores and Trading Company at Marine and 17th, acted as the first postmaster and was the second reeve. He even had plans for a golf course on his property, but the cost of land clearing and taxes proved too high to make it viable. He outfitted part of his barn with a gym, with hay cushioning the falls caused by any failed gymnastics moves. He remained active well into his later years; when the narrow catwalk for the Lions Gate Bridge was built, Lawson, then past seventy, walked it from the Capilano River to Stanley Park. Like many of the early developers,

Lawson had a strong sense of legacy, donating the land for the municipal hall for a dollar.

West Vancouver's dispersed geography and isolation from Vancouver made transportation crucial to its development. Keith Road provided essential east-west connections, but people also needed to get to Vancouver. Lawson began ferry service in 1906 from his 17th Street dock to the Columbia Street dock in today's Gastown. A group comprising

Between 1917 and 1930, massive western red cedars like this—more than three metres in diameter—were felled by hand on the slopes of Hollyburn Ridge and in the Capilano Valley. *West Vancouver Museum and Archives, 011.WVA.JOH*

Lawson, his brothers-in-law William Thompson and John Sinclair, and his colleague Robert McPherson formed the West Vancouver Transportation Company. Beginning November 8, 1909, this provided a more formal ferry service than Navvy Jack's ad hoc version and also enhanced the accessibility and value of his property. For ten cents, passengers could journey between West Vancouver and Vancouver on one of a little fleet that became an extension of the community. His partners gave Lawson the freedom to run the ferry company on the condition that he pay all the losses. These became considerable as the real estate prices started to slip, amounting to $11,500 by 1912, when he sold the *Seafoam*, the *West Vancouver* and a scow to the municipality for $6,500.

In 1913 the municipality built a wharf, ferry dock and Ferry Building at the foot of 14th Street on the relatively protected Ambleside

By 1914, West Vancouver's Ambleside had a few permanent buildings, a school (Hollyburn School is the dark roof, centre) and a great many stumps. Dreams of development would be on hold for several years, as the world, and Canada with it, went to war. *West Vancouver Museum and Archives, 020.WVA.LEY*

By 1981, the Ferry Building, once the hub of transportation in Ambleside, was a forlorn sight, leaning precariously on the edge of the waterfront, wedged between a roadway and a parking lot for buses. *West Vancouver Memorial Library, W. McPhee photo, 1028.WVML*

waterfront, which helped ensure that this would be the largest West Vancouver community. The Shamrock Tearooms, just west of the Ferry Building, became a popular meeting place, and for many years this part of the waterfront was one of the main focuses of the community. The Pacific Great Eastern Railway (PGE) commenced operations in 1914, and a bus service from about 1915 also provided community access from the Ferry Building.

With the opening of the Lions Gate Bridge, ferry traffic declined, and in 1947 the ferry run ended and the wharf was demolished. The Ferry Building became the public transit administrative office until 1986. The municipality declared it a heritage building in 1987, with Howard Yano Partners Architects drawing up plans for renovations. It is now a popular art gallery and community space mounting about twenty exhibitions annually, and is also the centre for the annual Harmony Arts Festival. A sport fishing pier, opened May 5, 1990, incorporates six man-made reefs designed to encourage marine growth near the pier and provide a refuge for fish.

Lawson's proud comment that "if it hadn't been for the ferries, there wouldn't have been a West Vancouver" may have been hyperbolic, but there is no doubt that ferries helped to make the municipal infrastructure viable. In the absence of any other transportation, a scow towed by one of the ferries was the only way for new settlers to move their household belongings to West Vancouver. They were also a social focus and an extension of the community. "Not the least enjoyable part of the trip for some of the commuters is a corner seat in the 'Smoking Cabin' where all local and world events of the day are settled....many a 'Debutante' and quite a few mature spinsters have, after getting tired of the wonderful scenery, started their courtship in the 'After Cabin.'"[23]

From 1908 to 1909, the Lower Mainland became the site of a land boom, although mostly this was pure speculation; few of those who purchased lots in West Vancouver actually moved here, providing landholders like Lawson with a lucrative market. Bill Chapman, who today operates Chapman Land Surveying Ltd., founded in 1906, recalls that in the early years the company would create as many as fifty lots a day; today a company might do twenty lots in a year. Investing in land became a local passion, but the speculative frenzy ended with a crash in 1913, with much of the land reverting to the municipality to cover unpaid taxes. By 1914 real estate prices had dropped by 25 per cent. A few years later, the lands the municipality acquired through tax sales made the massive British Properties development viable.

To the west of Ambleside, R.E. McNaughton—who had been born in India, taught at the University of Tasmania and McGill, and now enjoyed a professorship in Greek at UBC—acquired the land between 22nd and 28th Streets from the waterfront up to the current Upper Levels Highway. About 1910 he suggested the name of Dundarave for the area, based on his ancestral home in Scotland. The West Vancouver version's beachfront made this the most popular resort destination in the early days. Dundarave Pier was built at the foot of 24th Street for $40,000, with the Dundarave Regatta attracting visitors from far afield for athletic competitions and socializing.

The Mahon family acquired the land between 28th and 31st Streets on Dundarave's western border. This became Altamont, named after John Mahon's brother-in-law, who was Earl of Altamont from 1903 to

1913. The well-treed winding streets and large lots make this one of the most exclusive residential areas in West Vancouver. Edward Mahon also purchased the southern quarter of D.L. 763 on the southeastern corner of West Vancouver in 1910. Here Japanese carpenters built him a log house similar to the Teahouse at the Capilano Suspension Bridge, which with additions remains the centre of that community today.

Marine Drive, the contorted backbone of West Vancouver, now winds its leisurely way across the North Shore. A bus service, initiated in 1913, facilitated access. As settlers moved in, the route was developed; BC premier Richard McBride opened the section of Marine Drive to Caulfeild in 1915 (Marine Drive skirts the northern edge of the original Caulfeild). Other roads opened up more sections of the community, with almost ten kilometres of hard surfacing added every year from 1925. By 1929, ninety-six kilometres of open roads existed, about half of which were paved or hard surfaced. The plank roads and rock-strewn streets became history and cars blurred the boundaries between the communities. The PGE supplemented the roads with a commuter rail service from 1914 to 1928, stringing together the communities like the lights on a Christmas tree.

Francis Caulfeild was one of the early developers of the picturesque cove that he named after himself, purchasing extensive property in 1899. Captain Frank Kettle and his wife Mary shared his property, inhabiting the pilot house for many years; in 1910 Mary Kettle took over Caulfeild's first home as the local store, where many enjoyed her superb pumpkin pie. Caulfeild's daughter Dorothy recalls: "Many will remember him [Caulfeild] . . . pausing to gaze at the horizon with his eyes screwed up in a characteristic way, considering deeply the exactly right and most natural curve for the projected road to take." He sold lots to a select group of British compatriots, such as wholesale merchant and Vancouver Art Gallery patron Henry Stone, whose values he felt would be consistent with his vision of Caulfeild as a place where culture, elegance and natural beauty created a pastoral paradise. He presented land for the enjoyment of later West Vancouverites that became Klootchman Park, just north of Lighthouse Park, and Caulfeild Park, stretching along the waterfront east from near Caulfeild wharf for a kilometre. He also donated the land for St. Francis-in-the-Woods Church and a convalescent home.

Still farther west, in 1900, the well-known North Vancouver hotelier Pete Larson acquired a Crown Grant for D.L. 771—223 acres for a reported $370.50. This included all the waterfront from a point north of the west end of Eagle Island to Garrow Bay. He stipulated that a stopping point and station for the PGE be provided at his ranch, produce from which was sent to his two hotels in North Vancouver. Apparently business could have been better. In 1926, General Robert P. Clark and Frank Merrick, the latter a principal in the investment firm of Gillespie, Hart and Todd, acquired Larson's land for the unpaid taxes of $100,000. Clark developed and marketed a number of seaside lots on this land. Part of the land became the site of Gleneagles Golf Course, opened in June 1927, which still flourishes today, a scenic nine-hole layout.

Away on the western end of West Vancouver nestles Horseshoe Bay, a small community now sometimes seeing itself as West Vancouver's forgotten corner—or from another perspective, it's West Vancouver's western gateway. Gustav and Matilda Roedde, from Germany and Denmark respectively, via Cleveland, happened on Horseshoe Bay about 1908, acquiring two acres of land on which they located their ready-made house, towed in by a scow. Son Gus Roedde recalled that at that time, "All we needed to catch a salmon was a hand line, a chunk of lead and a Siwash spinner."[24] In 1909, Colonel Albert Whyte, a Philadelphia lawyer and land developer, acquired an extensive 2,100 acres for his West Shore & Northern Land Company, hoping to cash in on the land boom. Building lots for White Cliff City were laid out from Horseshoe Bay to Whytecliff, but within a few years burdensome taxes led him to mortgage his interests; his financial difficulties led to foreclosure. A more successful project by Major General Victor Odlum saw the development of his 35-acre estate. He bequeathed 4.77 acres to UBC, a property that, in 1988, became the nineteen single-family lots from which Cressey Developments created the gated community of Odlum Court.

Sunny Days and Peaceful Nights

> There is an old saying, "See Naples and die." We would rather ask the stranger to "come to West Vancouver and live."
> —*The West Vancouver News*, July 26, 1929

The intent of West Vancouver's founding fathers was, from the first, the building of a community of upscale homes. An April 1912 article in *B.C.*

Magazine foresaw that the council would "ensure that it retain the character of a high-class residential district." Many earlier visitors ignored this intent, enjoying laid-back pastimes and summer camping on the waterfront. In 1922, Dundarave had only three hundred permanent residents, but a summer population of a thousand. Summer visitors pitched tents, dismantling them in the fall, later adding walls and roofs. Jack Cruickshank and his five friends, for example, pitched a tent at 17th Street and Fulton Avenue in 1918, where the municipal hall now stands, dismantling it each winter but leaving the framework. In 1920, they moved to the waterfront, five hundred metres west of Dundarave Pier. They called their home the Kennel, and themselves the Hounds, wearing maroon turtleneck sweaters that each sported a large yellow letter of the Hounds' name.

> The Gamages kept cows. Two black and white monsters that lived in a field across Marine Drive from the house. . . . if I were alone, those creatures would lower menacing, horned heads (I think they were horned) and pace deliberately toward me. Their intent was obviously murderous.[25]
>
> —Mrs. Greenwood

In an archived interview with former municipal clerk Rupert Harrison, Cruickshank recalled that "we had a little folding Decca gramophone and we had a lot of nice popular records at that time. And we used to get in the canoe and paddle up along the shore and play these records. And there were all kinds of campers along the shore and often they'd call us in for a cup of coffee and we'd go in." In another interview with Harrison, Mrs. Ruth Nesbitt described the semi-rural life in the 1920s. "All the cows absolutely followed the old man down the hill [to Ambleside Park], stopped the traffic on Marine Drive and they just followed him right the way down. And then at 5 we went down to get them every day. We'd stand on the end of the slough down there and call, 'hey bossy, bossy' and they'd come."

For those with a taste for fresh food, the land was a cornucopia. The Capilano offered good trout fishing, and Cypress Creek provided mountain trout. Grouse could be hunted on Hollyburn Ridge, and ducks in the Ambleside slough. Until about 1920, hunters could pursue deer on the slopes, bear up the canyon and mountain goat farther up the mountains.

The small communities of Fisherman's Cove and Eagle Harbour also became popular getaways for summer recreation. As Katie Carter, who would later drive the production of a history of Bowen Island, recalled, "I remember dancing on the deck [of Kolthammer's store] to the sound of a gramophone playing 'Moonlight and Roses.'" The beaches attracted numerous visitors and boasted an Olympic standard diving platform with one-, three-, five- and ten-metre boards attracting thrill seekers and providing a venue for swimming and diving competitions. A replica of the Parthenon by restaurateur Nick Kogas perched for a number of years on a rocky outcrop before its demolition, but the area is now better known for its large marina.

> When the Chinese peddlers used to come around to the house, they'd have two baskets, one on each end of the pole and they would come to the door and they'd fillet the fish right there on the lid of their basket.[26]
>
> —Mrs. Greenwood

Local developer Fred Russell arranged the purchase of the properties for the West Vancouver Yacht Club from Frank Erridge, one of two brothers who owned two key lots in Fisherman's Cove where the club was planning to build. A chat on the dockside between the two ended with an agreement on the price, with Russell paying Erridge a dollar to seal the deal. The Thunderbird Marina was established December 21, 1945, the cove being dredged to make it an excellent harbour. Over in Eagle Harbour, the Smith home became the clubhouse for the Eagle Harbour Yacht Club, founded in 1969. West Vancouver now has more boats over ten metres than any other community on the Pacific coast.

> From Easter to Thanksgiving Miss Whitlaw and Miss McManus ran their store at Fisherman's Cove. Miss Whitlaw made the fruit pies and Miss McManus the meat, while Helen Holte did the dough. The store closed in 1958 when the Black Ball car ferries moved in to Horseshoe Bay.
>
> —*Bowen Island Undercurrent Second Annual Heritage Edition*, [ca. 199–]

Other popular vacation spots in the 1920s and '30s included Horseshoe Bay and Whytecliff Park. Dan and Eva Sewell arrived in Horseshoe

Bay in 1931, the same year BPP initiated its venture. For over eighty years, the multiple generations of the Sewells have been central to creating the community of Horseshoe Bay. They initiated the salmon derby, which with boating and other social activities attracted diverse celebrities like Bing Crosby, Gordie Howe and John Diefenbaker for fishing and summer fun. Today the Sewells are pivotal figures in a major new apartment development. Carol and Gary Troll of Troll's restaurant, along with other families, provided a continuity that engendered a strong identity in Horseshoe Bay. The relative remoteness of the community also allowed for other activities: during US prohibition years, Larson Bay (near Horseshoe Bay) served as a depot for a large amount of liquor smuggled south of the border.

For more vigorous play, many followed Rudolph Verne's footsteps and headed farther up the mountain to Hollyburn for some fine skiing and hiking. BC's Cypress Provincial Park and the Hollyburn area have provided a magnificent venue over the past century for summer and winter outdoor activities. Reeve Joe Leyland keenly supported local

Built in 1950 by Scandinavian craftsmen for Mr. and Mrs. Bert Baker, the Challenger Inn represented the high point of the cabin culture on Hollyburn. *West Vancouver Memorial Library, 1179.WVML*

athletic enterprises, first donating a cup to be awarded annually to the combined skiing champion in A class, and later, in 1936, officially opening the BC Skiing Championships on Hollyburn. Many skiers competed both locally and internationally, with Tom Mobraaten acquitting himself respectably in the 1936 Winter Olympics. Ski jumping was especially popular until the 1960s.

The extensive cabin area dates back at least to 1904, when George Marr built his cabin. Although many of the early cabins were little more than glorified tree forts built by adolescent boys, which have long since returned to the forest, many of the later cabins, often crafted from logs that had been cut to create the ski runs, have endured as a legacy of the skiing community. Scandinavian skiers who arrived in Canada in the 1920s often fashioned cabins from the yellow cedar that abounded at higher levels. During the Great Depression, the growing number of unemployed constructed much-needed cheap accommodation. The number of cabins grew to 250 by 1936, and perhaps to as many as 300 by the time the Second World War started.

This is the only surviving cabin area in the Lower Mainland; about a hundred structures continue to provide idyllic rural refuges. Most are eighty to ninety years old; no new cabins have been built since 1965. These are cabins in the true sense, with no electricity or other urban conveniences, and they have survived when other cabin areas on Grouse and Seymour Mountains and elsewhere have gradually disappeared. The high community profiles of many of the cabin owners and other Hollyburn habitués have helped with this. Sculptor Jack Harman received the Order of Canada in 1996 for his accomplishments, which include the statue of Roger Bannister and John Landy at the Pacific National Exhibition (PNE), and of Harry Jerome in Stanley Park. James Sinclair was a prominent Liberal MP and even better known as Margaret Trudeau's father (and Justin's grandfather). A dedicated group of community activists, led by Don Grant, has ensured that this legacy will not die. Hollyburn Lodge, the only surviving ski lodge on the North Shore, has recently been restored for the enjoyment of future generations. The trails in this area form one of the most popular cross-country ski venues in North America.

In 2014, the Upper Lands Working Group's suggestion of possibly phasing out the cabin leases raised howls of protest from the cabin owners and others, who pointed out their embodiment of the spirit of West Vancouver's harmony with nature. As their Statement of Significance says,

"The cabins exist in harmony with the creeks, wetlands and subalpine forest that is this place.... The cabin community is culturally significant because of its association with people and events related to the emerging ski culture on the north shore." So far, their position is being respected.

Hollyburn Mountain was a four-season playground for the outdoor community in the 1950s, as this well-attended regatta shows. *West Vancouver Memorial Library, 1278. WVML*

Maria (Kawamoto) Katsumi graduated from Inglewood High School in 1941. After the war the government gave her the choice of returning to Japan or moving east of the Rocky Mountains. Her parents chose the former, she the latter. However, the pull of West Vancouver was so strong that after fifty-three years of "exile" she returned, along with her husband, to West Vancouver.[27]

Maybe nostalgia colours our views of the past, but the pleasures of the waterfront, whether at Dundarave, Eagle Harbour or Horseshoe Bay, the camaraderie of Hollyburn skiing and the general sense of community surrounding life in West Vancouver do not exist in the same way today. Outdoor activities remain an attraction, but it's an older crowd and a quieter excitement. Younger people often head to Vancouver, or perhaps Whistler.

The Next Steps

While the communities of West Vancouver have developed separately, each has pursued similar patterns. The wandering cows and relaxed beach life of early years gradually disappeared from Ambleside and Dundarave in the 1920s and '30s, although a similar relaxed lifestyle (but mostly cowless) continued in the western communities through the '40s.

More stringent planning began in Ambleside and Dundarave in the 1950s, largely impelled by the business challenges presented by a growing Park Royal Shopping Centre. From the mid-'70s, concerted action took place to revitalize these communities. Finally, recent years have brought major developments to Ambleside, Horseshoe Bay and the western lands of the British Properties, as multi-unit residences have begun to replace many of the single-family homes, shaping the future of West Vancouver for decades to come.

For many years, the businesses of Ambleside and Dundarave existed in a cozy symbiosis with their local clientele. Some termed it a "Geritol shopping area," where people of a certain age enjoyed the convenience, value and personalized service and everybody (or at least quite a few) knew their name. Shoppers enjoyed dealing with someone who was a fellow member of the community. It was a place where commerce wasn't dominated by chain store prices and the high rents associated with locations in large malls. Early businesses included Crack Pots (where people could make their own pottery) and Mike Ibrahim's Barber Shop (where customers could enjoy the World Cup and other soccer matches). Most merchants were independent owners, content to enjoy the modest returns of their small stores.

After mid-century, as Park Royal grew and siphoned off much of their business, these shops and their owners came to recognize the need for new ways, although many of their long-time customers were quite happy with the way things were. These areas have mostly avoided (so far) the drastic clear-cutting of older buildings that has decimated many of the communities in other parts of the Lower Mainland. The old-growth generally remains, although some have fallen victim to the onslaught of newer buildings.

Whereas Park Royal was designed for a car culture, Ambleside and Dundarave developed as pedestrian-oriented communities. So when cars came to be the drivers of development, the lack of parking and the distances between shops spread out along Marine Drive became a definite disadvantage for shoppers, especially for some of the older customers. The 1956 Ambleside District Planning Study noted that Ambleside was still the main shopping area for West Vancouver, but called for more parking and changes to make this area more accessible to the shopper. But Park Royal was hot on its heels, and by 1970 had eclipsed Ambleside as the main commercial area in spite of the numerous potential shoppers living in the newly minted adjacent apartments. Increased traffic raised concerns. In 1964, some thought of turning Marine Drive through Ambleside into a one-way street going west.

A 1975 planning report for Ambleside by architects Ian Davidson and Daryl Foreman recommended a major reconfiguring to appeal to diverse ages, with pedestrian malls revitalizing the environment. Buildings would be limited to three or four stories but include a mix of commercial, office and residential space. Dundarave had similar needs, in response to which architect Ray Olson suggested an imaginative filling out of West Vancouver with office buildings—not a popular option.

What actually happened was modest, although still substantial. First out of the gate, in 1976, Dundarave reached an agreement with the UBC School of Community and Regional Planning: twenty-one students, divided into three groups (headed respectively by Harry Lash, former director of planning for the GVRD, and UBC professors Michael Seeling and Paul Roer), would study the community. Cutbacks and a total review of the program by Victoria slowed the pace of change, but by 1984 serious plans for the regeneration of both Ambleside and Dundarave began to coalesce, with most construction taking place in the summer of 1988. Architect Karl Gustavson's plans for Dundarave included new sidewalks, curbs, trees and planters. Old-fashioned lamps with black tops carried on down 24th Street to the waterfront to link the two. Seating and bus stop enclosures recognized the needs of an older clientele. Former mayor Mark Sager's father suggested plants for the divider on Marine Drive. More parking was added, although there is never enough of that. The merchants and the municipality shared the costs on a 75/25 basis.

A major refurbishing of Ambleside took place in the summers of 1988 and 1989. Under the guidance of landscape architect Don Vaughan, streets were rebuilt with a six-foot-wide (two-metre) concrete sidewalk on Marine Drive, with telephone and hydro wires placed underground. Benches provided seating and new trees shaped the area's aesthetic value, while old-fashioned street lamps enhanced the village's traditional character. On 14th Street, a park-like character, more variety and a link with the waterfront added to the overall effect. All north-south streets from 13th to 19th were upgraded.

A place to socialize and have a drink after a busy day does not seem an outlandish wish, but few proposals raise the ire of some of West Vancouver's citizens like the idea of a neighbourhood pub. When John Wiechold proposed in 2000 to change his Dundarave Café to a sixty-five-seat neighbourhood pub, the opposition mustered in full force. Nightmares of noise, illegal parking and proximity to Irwin Park Elementary School (but wouldn't their times be different?) mobilized many of the residents. Erwen Smith spearheaded the Friends of Dundarave Improvement Society (FDIS) and attended meetings where council discussed the proposal. His comments—"I've heard about the vomit and the smell of urine"—brought gasps of horror from a mostly older audience. West Vancouver councillor Liz Byrd had less sympathy. "In Dundarave one can roll a bowling ball down the sidewalks and not hit a single person." This pub proposal went no further, although in a few subsequent establishments a drink may indeed be purchased.

Most new development moved farther west. From 1973, a number of developers cast hungry eyes on the 280 acres of pristine Caulfeild Plateau. This was the largest undeveloped area below the Upper Levels Highway,

Contrary to its name, there is very little about Caulfeild Plateau that is level. Not subject to the usual rules regarding setbacks and square footage, clusters of houses perch where they can gain footholds, sometimes cantilevering over rocky outcrops. *Photo by John Moir*

stretching from Marine Drive to the Upper Levels Highway between Caulfeild Drive and Nelson Creek. The largest landowner, Howard Martin of Westmount Estates with 106.52 acres, had been developing land in the Caulfeild area since 1931. In 1954, he donated a ten-acre site for Caulfeild School, stipulating that the eastern end of the property be kept forested as he believed children should have contact with nature. After his death in 1994, four charities received bequests totalling $27 million, including $3.6 million to the West Vancouver Community Foundation.

Other property holders in this area included the British Properties, Rutland Estates, Seaview Estates, MacKechnie Estates and Caulfeild Estates. The land that became the Caulfeild area was developed through a land-use contract rather than the standard subdivision development.

This contract, which set out site-specific land uses and conditions of development, laying out the density, roads and parkland, was intended to eliminate the problems associated with trying to relate flat-land zoning techniques to hillside locations; it also gave council greater control over the details. Peter Jones, who became mayor in 1974, played a key role in implementing these changes.

Surveyor Bill Chapman described the Whytecliff development as being in concentric circles. The central area had three units per acre, then five, then eight as development moved outward. Some of the lots were quite small, only thirty-three feet (ten metres), but a large amount of green space compensated for this density. The green space was increased to 15 per cent rather than the standard 5 per cent, but overall the density remained at three units per acre. Three lively public meetings in April and May 1978 gave the local ratepayers a venue to express their vigorous concerns about density, green belt area, water and drainage, public transportation and traffic volume.

The development went ahead with some minor modifications, although concern continued about large houses on the thirty-three-foot (ten-metre) lots. And then there was the problem of blasting, which permanently changed the terrain and sometimes sent errant boulders crashing down the steep slopes. In 1983, the home of Reinhard and Doreen Doreth at the 4800 block of Keith Road received two direct hits from 40- and 50-pound (18- and 23-kg) boulders: "An unfortunate mistake" came the cavalier response from the blasting company. But mostly rocks stayed where they should, and in 1985 the development received the Governor General's Award for design. In the end, roughly 2,000 new residents more than doubled the population of Caulfeild. In 1986, the thirty-two-townhome development of Edenshaw, a part of this development, overcame the challenges of a rocky site to be named that year's Best Residential Development in BC.

To the west lie Fisherman's Cove and Eagle Harbour—places of spectacular beauty even by West Vancouver standards, where lush forest shrouds houses often perched on impossible cliffsides. For the most part, this area has not suffered the excessive tree cutting that has decimated the landscape in many other locales. Cove Crest Subdivision, operated by Community Investments Co. Ltd., developed thirty acres here in 1955, but municipal council and local groups have successfully resisted most extensive building plans. At various times from 1973, the International Land Corporation promoted a number of luxury waterfront developments, but none materialized. BC Railway had plans to build forty homes on their right-of-way, but vigorous reactions from the local citizenry convinced the municipality to preserve it as open space. Residents found it more acceptable when a French restaurateur opened an elegant eatery in 1971, purveying everything from steak-and-kidney pies at 55¢ to escargots cooked in brandy for $1.25.

Still farther west, Horseshoe Bay's growth largely depended on new transportation links such as the PGE (from 1914) and the Upper Levels Highway (from 1957). Unfortunately, as a local commuter railway, the PGE's reliance on passenger revenue over the more lucrative freight business at a 5:1 ratio led to its decline after 1921. The opening of the Second Narrows Bridge in 1925 improved road connections, increasing road competition with the railway. Although the railway closed on November 29, 1928, the right-of-way was retained and the rail service was revived in the 1950s, but not as a commuter line, so it did not serve Horseshoe Bay. A bylaw prohibiting locomotives from sounding their whistles in Ambleside and Dundarave preserved the peaceful days and nights of their residents.

The arrival of the Black Ball Ferry Line in 1951 signalled the end of Horseshoe Bay as a fishing paradise and the beginning of its new life as a minor port and a more permanent residential community. Its image as party central gradually faded as it became a staging area for the ferries, and the salmon sought cleaner waters. A 1954 planning study noted a need for more housing to be filled by rezoning to allow more duplexes. Many summer cottages built between 1921 and 1930 needed replacing. With the development of the highway up to Squamish, it became less of a residence for short-term marine and mine workers, and more of a stable white-collar, professional community.

In 1974 George Osborne of the Municipal Planning Commission expressed concern that "Horseshoe Bay is deteriorating and will become a slum if something isn't done soon." A totem pole carved by Chief William Jeffries and his son Rupert was raised in Horseshoe Bay Park in 1975, but the refurbishment of the community's seaside commercial core did not take place until 1986. At that time, paver blocks replaced old sidewalks, streets underwent repair, and new street lamps and public benches were installed. Traffic patterns were redesigned, and a new public square was established with a ten-foot (three-metre) ship's propeller as its focal point. The Horseshoe Bay Community Association received $80,000 from the sale of the Horseshoe Bay Community Hall to developers, which funded the development of a $40,000 water park.

The Shape of the Future

Since 2000, West Vancouver has explored different directions in attempts to bring a greater affordability to a community that is literally pricing itself out of the market. Houses are still being demolished at a rate driven by the windfall profits to be made from building their huge replacements. Although the municipality's population has been stable, house demolitions in West Vancouver have averaged 102 each year over the past ten. Many heritage and character homes have been victims of projects that, with the inflation of land prices, have been lucrative indeed. But larger lots are on occasion being reimagined to provide "gentle densification," and larger projects are providing the relative economies of apartment living without some of the negative aspects of constraint in a monolithic tower.

In recent years, the municipality has searched for ways to preserve some of its architectural treasures while providing more living spaces. In 2007, the Merrick House in Eagle Harbour was slated for demolition. Architectural writer Adele Weber described the uniqueness of this house: "It seems to emerge right out of an old-growth tree, suggesting a Tolkienesque forest mansion with its cantilevered rooms, Gothic domes and rotunda poking into the treetops." Its front door was the recycled drafting table of legendary modernist architect Ron Thom. The municipality suggested subdividing the 11,000-square-foot lot and building a small house on the new lot, in character with the original house. In exchange, the original house would be designated as a heritage property and hence be protected. Although this would likely have a negative effect on its value because it would limit the owner's ability to make changes, the value of the additional lot and house would substantially increase the value of the property as a whole. This proposal was accepted.

Most infill residences created in this way sell for well over $2 million. Clearly, this is not a way to develop affordable housing, but to preserve character and heritage houses while providing some lower-cost residences and addressing some community needs, which were ignored by too many developments of the 1980s and '90s. Developer Michael Geller has worked with heritage consultant Don Luxton and others on a number of sites to preserve the original house by allowing additional structures. The process includes working with the municipality to analyze the value of building sites and recommending what can be preserved. This can include both exterior and interior features.

The craftsman-style bungalow built at 1425 Gordon in 1913 for Valient Vivian Vinson, a well-known photographer and reeve of West Vancouver, exemplifies successful application of this process. In the Upper Hollyburn area, the original structure of the first house has been preserved and divided into two units. The addition of a laneway cottage and a garden cottage takes advantage of the spacious lot, so four residences incorporate and replace the original single one. The new structures echo some of the features of the old, with the gardens recreating some of the original Edwardian landscape character (no bamboo allowed).

Other properties that have been or are in the process of being similarly developed include the Sutherland residence at 1768 Inglewood (Burgers Architecture, 1927), the Toby residence at 2055 Queens (architect Ray Toby, 1961), the Staples residence at 6985 Isleview Road (Erickson/Massey 1966–67), the Sykes residence at 5616 Westport Place (architect Peter Kaffka, 1964) and the Binning residence (designed by B.C. Binning with the assistance of architects Ned Pratt and R.A.D. Berwick, 1941). Constructed without government money, the new infill buildings in these projects can add considerably to property value. Luxton has noted that "topography is our friend" in West Vancouver, as sloping lots often allow for the building of additional structures without sacrificing views from the original building. The delicate process—which includes consultations with neighbours and collaboration between the municipal government and developers, whose agendas are not always the same—seems to be working.

Other houses have fared less well. In Horseshoe Bay, architect Arthur Erickson made ingenious use of a steep, rocky slope by contouring the Graham House to the shape of the cliff against which it was built. This represents the only time to date that *Life* magazine (1968) featured a Vancouver architect. Warren Beatty and Julie Christie rented it when filming *McCabe & Mrs. Miller* in West Vancouver in 1970. But it met with the wrecker's ball in 2007; opinion differs as to whether structural problems justified this action.

Townhouses and row housing have been built with increasing frequency in West Vancouver: the total of semi-detached houses, row houses and duplexes in the 2016 census came to 2,390. Many replaced single-family homes, although their high cost meant most were more likely to be bought by empty nesters than young families.

In 2010, following public input, Geller Properties Ltd. took over a rezoning application from Bowling Green Townhomes Ltd. for three blocks on Esquimalt Avenue at 21st Street. On July 4, 2011, council amended the OCP to allow construction of nine units, including six duplexes and three coach houses, on these three lots. In 2013 Michael Geller developed the Hollyburn Mews on Esquimalt Avenue for people who "want to downsize but not downgrade." The inspiration comes from early twentieth-century West Vancouver seaside cottages, and the concept creates a neighbourhood within a neighbourhood. With a lush meandering mews that separates duplexes and coach houses, this development aims to bridge the gap between single-family homes and apartments while fitting in with the traditional character of West Vancouver neighbourhoods.

However, this development did not happen without a struggle, as some feared this could introduce "spot zoning" and increased density into single-family neighbourhoods. Perhaps it is a slippery slope, but it seems like a slope the community is cautiously navigating in its attempt to provide relatively affordable spaces for young couples and families, a demographic sorely lacking in West Vancouver. But at the same time, the number of places to build infill housing or townhouses is limited.

Other projects have brought much greater density to central areas of West Vancouver. Some of the earliest houses in the British Properties went up just behind what became Park Royal North, on Evelyn Drive—Evelyn of the Guinness family. But the prominence of the area's namesake did not save the houses from deteriorating to the point that a half century later the locals began referring to it as the Dogpatch of West Vancouver (a relative term). The 2001–02 OCP designated this twenty-four-acre area as a special study area for multiple homes.

Millennium Corporation commenced the expensive and time-consuming endeavour of purchasing the fifty-five single-family homes for development, and by the end of 2006 most residents had sold their homes and moved out. In the meantime, some members of the community mounted determined opposition to the plan. Fear of increased traffic, pollution, loss of sea views and a negative effect on property values culminated in two vigorous meetings in early July 2005. Shortly after, the proposal lost in council by one vote. Control was turned back to the community, and after much discussion council approved revised plans in 2007. But the expense of carrying this project eventually became too much for Millennium, whose difficulties were compounded by the 2008 recession and their ill-fated Olympic Village on False Creek. In 2011, Millennium defaulted on a $72-million mortgage and both the Evelyn development and the Olympic Village went into receivership.

Onni purchased the Evelyn project that year, achieving much more success. Their development, inspired by Arthur Erickson's architectural vision, was planned as "a showcase for West Vancouver's commitment to sustainability and innovation" with terraced glass walls cascading down the hillside. Five six-storey buildings contain 349 units. Onni is returning to the properties' roots in consciously invoking the spirit of West Coast modernism, but adapting it to apartment living: "With an absence of unnecessary ornaments, Evelyn utilizes a combination of raw natural materials that fit within its environment, creating beauty that is unique to its setting and embracing nature." And (just in case you might need it)

The Onni development, seated on the hillside between Park Royal North and more traditional single-family homes above, is incorporating high-end, higher-density living into the landscape. *Photo by John Moir*

each unit features a Sub-Zero wine cooler to chill your wine. The tiered apartments echo those of Panorama Village a little farther west (but with more greenery) and the recent Grosvenor development on Marine Drive.

The Grosvenor complex, two six- and seven-storey blocks of commercial and apartment space on the 1300 block of Marine Drive, is another major project reconfiguring the face of downtown West Vancouver. Designed by K.M. Cheng, who was mentored by Arthur Erickson, like the Evelyn development, it invokes the modernist principles of an earlier generation. It intends to provide "a new vision of Ambleside in the heart of West Vancouver," an outdoor living room for the community. The architecture adopts the strong horizontal terrace form and incorporates substantial landscape elements such as green roofs and terrace gardens. Vigorous opposition came from those who felt that the proposed large buildings impinged on the cozy ambience of the small Ambleside shops. Some said that there was too much retail in Ambleside already, whereas others feared that non-residents would purchase most of the units, leading to an influx of buyers from outside West Vancouver. Other criticism came from those who thought a twenty-storey high-rise would disrupt the view of fewer than those affected by the current building's more longitudinal configuration.

Supporters argue that it will engender a 10 to 16 per cent rise in Ambleside business, giving the quiet community a much-needed wake-up call. Buyers quickly snapped up a total of ninety-nine condo and retail units in the first building, which are expected to generate $1 million a year in added tax revenue. The second building will have forty-two new homes. The apartments are modest in size, split fairly equally between those under 1,500 square feet, those 1,500–2,500, and those over 2,500. A Douglas Coupland sculpture called *The Best Day Forever* recalls beachcombing on the waterfront, and paintings by well-known local artist Gordon Smith will also be featured. A 650-square-metre glazed pedestrian galleria operated by Artists for Kids Trust will join the two buildings and provide a public plaza. A ten-year partnership with Kay Meek Centre to support local programming will include performances at Grosvenor Square.

Since about 2000, the magic of community amenity contributions has gone a long way toward softening the hearts of those opposed to development. The soaring price of real estate, particularly in West Vancouver, has meant that developers are willing to make substantial contributions in cash or in kind in exchange for an increase in the allowable square footage or density in their developments. About 75 per cent of the increased value from higher zoning density goes back to the community, while the remaining 25 per cent acts as a risk buffer in the (unlikely) event that value will decline.

A $700,000 portion from the Hollyburn Mews project has been contributed to West Vancouver's affordable housing fund. A bonus of $11.3 million from the Grosvenor development, as well as the $46 million sale of the old police building on the Grosvenor site, has enabled the municipality to pay cash for Vancouver Coastal Health's $16-million parcel at 2195 Gordon, previously owned by the BC government; it also funded the new police building adjacent to the municipal hall. As a bonus for being allowed to build beyond the normal allowable density, the new development of Westbank in Horseshoe Bay contributed $10.7 million to the community amenities fund. This will pay for a boardwalk and a new boathouse with $4 million set aside to defray the costs of future affordable housing.

Yet Westbank has also proven controversial. Beginning about 2009, long-time West Vancouver resident Dan Sewell discussed with architect Paul Merrick ways of giving Horseshoe Bay a major makeover. About 2014, Westbank Projects became actively involved with generating the plans, which now comprise six high-rise, mid-rise and low-rise buildings, with 159 apartments from 570 to 3,000 square feet. Designed by Merrick Architecture, it is partly inspired by Portofino, a hillside fishing village that overlooks a small harbour on the Italian Riviera, and is slated for completion in 2019.

Many local residents initially welcomed this development as a way of rejuvenating the area with more shops and people, and looked forward to selling their homes and moving in. The anticipation turned to disappointment for some when the unit costs revealed them to be far beyond the means of most locals. The project also faced delays after West Vancouver learned the company was actively marketing the project in Hong Kong even before it was approved by council. Westbank then agreed to focus its initial efforts on local residents, giving West Vancouverites a 5 per cent discount; new residents must sign a declaration saying they will live in the unit, which should help limit absentee owners, and a clause in the agreement states that the strata council cannot restrict rentals. The move to give preference to locals, the first of its kind in the Vancouver area, is commendable, although it remains to be seen how effectively it will be enforced. And the music in the promotional video has an unmistakably Chinese cadence.

In his 2009 book *Dream City*, Vancouver commentator and writer Lance Berelowitz discusses how zoning, although it has acted as a salutary check on unbridled development, "is by definition exclusionary, limiting things to a preordained set of possibilities."[28] He favours creating areas where more flexible zoning will allow the creation of a "city of desire." "Serendipity, complexity, imagination, surprise and delight are what great cities offer." Greater "character, colour and value" could flow from the introduction of mixed-use developments, as have developed in many older cities. A coffee shop in your apartment lobby? Why not?

The Green Necklace of Parks

> For those who cannot travel, free admission to the best scenery of their neighbourhood is desirable.
>
> —Frederick Law Olmsted

In *Who's Your City?* urbanist Richard Florida discusses the importance of place as a contributor to human happiness; especially significant is physical beauty and aesthetic appeal. "Places that rank high in aesthetics and openness . . . level the playing field for all their residents. . . . The aesthetics of a place—its physical beauty and natural amenities—are public goods that we can all use and enjoy."[29] "People are drawn to and pay more for that which is more aesthetically pleasing."[30]

From its earliest days, West Vancouver has had the foresight to develop a park system that enshrines its natural beauty. Early settlers such as John Lawson and Francis Caulfeild laid the foundation for this system through their donations of land to the community. In 2006, West Vancouver had between 151 and 161 parks, providing more parkland per capita than any other BC community, while the immense backyard of the endless mountains to the north provides magical escapes for the weekend explorer.

The Board of Park Commissioners was created in 1943 to preserve the municipality's park-like setting. Its chair, Claire Downing, provided the option money and paid for the advertising that made seven waterfront parks possible, including Horseshoe Bay, Sandy Cove, West Bay and John Lawson. Former councillor Ted Baynes says that "he [Downing] was determined that the future generations have some parks and he was prepared to fight for them." J.E. Wood recalls that "if he goofed, he would take the money out of his own pocket and straighten it out." Baynes's friend Isaac Lipovsky put up the original money for Altamont Playground and gave it, with the tennis courts (the first two public courts in West Vancouver), to the municipality for a dollar.

The democratizing experience of public parks counters the elitism of high-priced real estate. As the 1978 Parks and Recreation Commission report states, "these have retained the essence of West Vancouver's village character: the large intensive use parks and the abundance of smaller parks and trails; neighbourhoods with their strong identities; narrow local roads with a minimum of sidewalks; the wealth of evergreen trees that abound in the residential areas."

In 1960, West Vancouver hired landscape architect Heinz Berger, who applied his rigorous German education and expertise in park development to make major additions to the park system. His first job was to design Glenmore Park, off the northeast tip of the British Properties. Although not part of that company's purchase, Glenmore's two hundred acres abuts its northeast edge and is geographically a part of the same area. During the 1930s it was part of a large parcel of land owned by the Greater Vancouver Water District. In 1937, when it was found to be outside the Capilano watershed, the parcel was created and title raised in the name of Mountain Park Limited. In June 1942, Toronto's Avista Ltd. obtained title.

Glenmore Development purchased the property in April 1954, with Alexander Browning as president and general manager. It remained a single-family development, with all sales made through Arnold Shook of Shook Realty. Extensive plans for a school, shopping centre and multiple family dwellings did not materialize.

Where the Glenmore shopping centre had been planned, Berger designed what was probably the first playscape in North America, including a baseball diamond and a roller skating rink. As he describes in his memoir, "On the northeast end I placed two tennis courts, and we had plenty of open lawn areas for informal play or picnics. A beautiful shallow creek ran through the middle of the park, which was a favorite unorganized play area. West of the creek, on a slight slope, I designed a ship's bridge playscape looking out over the water, with a real ship's steering wheel and a wading and spray pool."[31]

On projects such as the upgrading of Lawson Park in 1962, Berger consulted with local children to see what they would like in their new playground. He recalls that "after the meeting we built a large raft with big logs, with ladders up to the mast for climbing. And we built two flying saucers with an entrance and port holes, one large porthole on the top, with a fireman's pole for the junior astronauts to slide into the flying saucer."[32]

In Ambleside Park, Berger designed the first-ever water playground; in 1968, the city added the first-ever fitness circuit in North America, and in 1969 the first adventure playground. Like Lawson Park, the adventure playground grew from what the users—the children—wanted. Do we make playgrounds that please adults or children? Children built their own playhouses and developed their own gardens, with a lot of sawing and hammering. This created an apparent mess that some adults might not enjoy, but the children loved it. As with the best modernist houses, his structures responded organically to the natural surroundings and their builders' imaginations.

In the mid-'70s, with the help of Vancouver sculptor Nelson Holland, Berger designed the first skateboard facility in Canada, near the old Inglewood School; sadly, as it became a teenage hangout, it was later filled in and seeded with grass. Although skateboarding and long boarding are not allowed on West Vancouver streets, skateboard parks have been built in Ambleside Park and near the Gleneagles Community Centre.

Foreshore rights had been rejected in 1926, a prescient move that enabled public access to the waterfront, making West Vancouver's beautiful Centennial Seawalk possible. First proposed by councillor Don Lanskail in 1965, the Seawalk now attracts a multitude of visitors each year to enjoy its natural beauty. Some had argued for a beach rather than a sidewalk, a place to beachcomb, but the Seawalk won out. The first section opened in June 1967 from 24th to 23rd Streets. In the mid-'70s, under mayor Peter Jones, the municipality developed a policy to purchase thirty-two waterfront homes along Argyle between 14th and 18th Streets to add to the walk. Not all of the owners appreciated what some experienced as pressure to sell, but a more conciliatory approach later led to the purchase of their properties and the Seawalk's continued success. It has survived projects that would have prevented its completion, including recreational and commercial facilities and art galleries. Public access runs from Dundarave along the waterfront to the Capilano River and up to the Cleveland Dam, a unique legacy. Only two houses remain to be purchased, at a cost of $4 million each. On May 6, 2013, council voted to dedicate the entire waterfront from 13th to 18th Street as a park.

Other parks fill a variety of community needs. Ambleside Park, designated in 1918, is largely on land reclaimed from the swampy waterfront; in early days, the slough extended as far as 14th Street. The first development here was a baseball diamond at 13th and Marine in the 1930s. By 1940, that had become a rugby field, but during the Second World War the Department of National Defence leased the park. A swimming pool was added in 1954, and during the '60s the city used 88,000 cubic yards of fill to reclaim land south of the PGE. The bird sanctuary, pitch and putt, fitness circuit and Seawalk make this one of the most highly used parks in West Vancouver.

Lighthouse Park, leased from the federal government since May 1, 1910, on a series of twenty-one-year leases, conveys a more rugged grandeur, home to one of the last stands of virgin coastal timber in this part of the province. A lighthouse, built in 1912, replaced the earlier wooden structure Arthur Finney, a Nanaimo builder, had constructed in 1874. The park is an example of the transformation from coast-climax fir to hemlock forest, providing an outdoor classroom for biologists and arborculturalists. In 1963, Heinz Berger converted the smallest of the old army huts into a nature house; by scrounging unused equipment from the West Vancouver School Board, he set up a facility where summer students could give lectures and take visitors on nature walks. Over 60,000 visited annually, although Berger recalls that subsequent budget cuts arose from the fact that 60 per cent of users came from outside West Vancouver.

Still farther west, Whytecliff Park was first established as Rockcliffe Park when the Marine Drive extension from Caulfeild to Whytecliff opened in 1926. The original owner of this land, W.W. Boultbee, sold his estate to the Union Steamship Company in 1938. In 1953 the municipality purchased forty acres of the Union Steamship's land there and on Whyte Island to create a public park. Visitors could savour the original burgers made by Vera Hochfelder, whose business has become the popular Vera's Burgers chain. When the Teahouse burned down in 1962, Berger designed a viewpoint, but this later deteriorated and was destroyed. An underwater park opened nearby in 1973, and in 1992 the Vancouver Aquarium helped to create Whytecliff Marine Park, Canada's first marine protected area, which has become the most popular scuba diving area in the province.

In *Through the Trees*, Elspeth Bradbury discusses how trees enhance the mental and physical well-being of all who live in their presence. They grow fast in the benign climate of the West Coast, sometimes three metres a year, so a row of small decorative trees one year can block the views of neighbouring residents only a few years later, providing a potential hazard if their roots become unstable. If they block a resident's views of the harbour, they can reduce property values by hundreds of thousands of dollars. Some residents have gone so far as to make clandestine nighttime assaults to cut down or damage unwanted trees. A 1975 municipal report described the problem as a case of "private prerogative as opposed to public interests and public responsibilities," although it could also pit neighbour against neighbour.

Conflict erupted in 1979 between West Vancouverites who loved their trees and those who preferred their views (and their property values). Quoted in the *Vancouver Sun,* Alan Jessup, one of the original Bowen Island property owners, viewed a future dystopia in which armies of trees assumed control of the world: "We'll all be living in a dense rain forest in which sunlight and view will be eliminated. Real estate values are being eroded by the fact that many houses are having their view taken away from them by trees."[33] In the same article, lawyer Anne Sweeney took a more reasoned approach: "There's no right to light and view in common law or in B.C. or Canadian statutes,"[34] she said, but where trees (and real estate values) are concerned, reason often takes a back seat.

In his memoir, Heinz Berger described an encounter with the problems accompanying the coexistence of trees and people.

> *Often I had to mediate between neighbours to try to solve their tree problems. In one instance a family living in the British Properties had a fantastic view, but their neighbours south of them planted many native trees on their property. After some years they grew so tall that they blocked their neighbour's view. When they could not agree on what to do, I was asked to mediate. My suggestion was that the*

people who lost their view invite their neighbours and me for a cup of tea and show us pictures of their former fantastic view. After the tea and photos, we agreed that some thinning of trees would be beneficial. An arborist was hired and instructed what to do. But unfortunately he removed more trees than we all had agreed to. In the evening the owners arrived home from work, and all hell broke loose. The view people and I were sued. The final result—some new trees had to be replanted.[35]

Nature lovers often resent cutting trees for any purpose; in 1989, some objected to trees being cut at the new Cedardale Park, but as parks manager Frank Kurucz pointed out, "You can't play tennis where there are trees." In 1996, Shirley Charlton-Nicholson became the district's first full-time permanent arborist, in part to attempt a resolution by striking a judicious balance between the public and private. Some developers were reined in. In 1997, after the Cascadia Group, developers of Caulfeild's Rockcliffe, removed three trees from the greenbelt, they were required to pay $15,000 for replacement planting and donate $3,000 to the West Vancouver Community Foundation.

On April 20, 2016, public consultation led to the passing of an interim tree bylaw to regulate the cutting of trees on private lands. While this bylaw encourages a good-neighbour approach to resolving conflict on an amicable personal basis, it also strikes a balance between recognizing the importance of trees to the well-being of community residents while recognizing that safety and aesthetics sometimes require their removal. Residents expressed concerns that on some lots trees were being clear-cut before the new home was built. As a result, residents now need a permit to cut any tree with a diameter of 75 centimetres or more, which can still be a sizable tree. Some suggest that retaining tall trees has the advantage of reducing the apparent height of a building, making it appear more neighbourly.

For the 2010 Winter Olympics, the organizers wanted more safe and efficient highways to shuttle athletes, the media and spectators between Vancouver and Whistler. The winding road to Whistler, the scene of many serious accidents, received a major makeover, with one of the most controversial changes slated for Eagleridge Bluffs, adjacent to

The Eagle Bluffs protest camp of 2006 drew considerable media (and police) attention, as protestors clung to the native Arbutus trees in an effort to stop road construction for the 2010 Olympics through a much-loved nature area above Horseshoe Bay. *Photo by Mike Wakefield, NSNews*

Horseshoe Bay. A number of routes across the Bluffs were proposed; West Vancouver council and BPP supported a tunnel, which would minimize environmental impact. But when it came to decision time in 2004, the provincial government selected a much less environmentally friendly (but cheaper) four-lane overland route, in spite of massive evidence

West Vancouver has a remarkable endowment of land for community use.

Sandy Cove. *Photo by John Moir*

Top: John Lawson, second man from the left in the back row (in dark suit), hosts a church picnic in his field, ca. 1915. *West Van Archives, 0943.WVA.RAH*

Right: Paddleboarding at Whytecliff. *Photo by John Moir*

Bottom: Volleyball game at Ambleside. *Photo by John Moir*

Top: This tiny beach at 19th Street was created as part of a municipal shoreline protection initiative.

Middle left: Snowshoeing, Black Mountain.

Middle right: Scuba divers at Caulfeild.

Bottom right: Dundarave.

All photos by John Moir

Top: Smelt fishing, Ambleside. *Photo by John Moir*

Right: Watching a cruise ship at the mouth of the Capilano River. *Photo by John Moir*

Bottom: Eagle Harbour beach, ca. 1928. *West Van Archives 3038. WVA.PHO*

Above: Musicians at the Harmony Arts Festival, 2015. *Photo by John Moir*

Below: The Spirit Trail, Ambleside. *Photo by John Moir*

Top: Hollyburn Pavilion, corner of 17th Street and Bellevue, was West Van's first community centre, hosting a rollerdrome and dance floor, ca. 1935. *West Van Archives, 3410.WVA.PHO*

Above: West Vancouver Art Museum, formerly the Gertrude Lawson house, holds the West Van Archives and a gallery of art and design. *Photo by John Moir*

Right: The Coho Festival every September is a major community event. *Photo by John Moir*

Top left: Gleneagles Community Centre.

Top right: West Vancouver Community Centre.

Left: Hollyburn Lodge.

Bottom: The War Memorial Cenotaph stands across from West Vancouver Memorial Library.

All photos by John Moir

Top: This illustration shows the proposed Cypress Village area for the British Properties.
Illustration by Urban Design Associates

Right: British Properties reps bring their proposals to the public in Ambleside.
Photo by John Moir

Below: As West Van develops over the next century, careful stewardship will be needed to maintain the legacy of public space.
Illustration courtesy Grosvenor Americas

from the scientific and environmental communities on the damage this would cause.

The swift and intense opposition comprised an unusual alliance of diverse protesters, including the Squamish people, who joined the British Properties and the municipality in fighting hard for a four-lane tunnel. Four hundred community residents turned out to a town hall meeting at Gleneagles. Urbanist Jane Jacobs wrote her support: "I wish to convey my support and admiration to the people of West Vancouver who are sacrificing their time, energy and possibly even their freedom to preserve and protect the magnificent and irreplaceable Eagleridge Bluffs and Lawson Creek wetlands from this destructive ill-conceived scheme." Many saw this as a symbol of corporate greed trampling environmental concerns and the wishes of the people.

West Vancouver mayor Pamela Goldsmith-Jones joined a number of others in posing partially nude for the 2005 Back the Bluffs calendar. On May 25, 2006, at a protest that included Jacobs's son Ned, police arrested twenty-three protesters. Several were jailed, including well-known activist Betty Krawczyk and Squamish elder Harriet Nahanee, both past seventy. Nahanee died of pneumonia and undiagnosed lung cancer shortly following her nine-day incarceration. Krawczyk, who had defied a court injunction to stay away from the site of highway construction, served seven months of a ten-month sentence. A new four-lane, 2.4-kilometre section of the Sea-to-Sky Highway now slices through sensitive wetlands.

Although attempts by West Vancouverites to protect the community's natural environment have generally been more successful, preservation must be balanced by the need to accommodate more people in a community with little undeveloped space. The question of preserving natural beauty while providing space for additional people has both ethical and practical dimensions. Ethically, what are West Vancouver's responsibilities to accommodate more residents? Practically, how can the price of these accommodations be kept within reason? The ongoing debates surrounding these issues are shaping West Vancouver's future.

Lost in the heart of the old Squamish territory . . . there is a silent power which for centuries was reflected in the spirit of the people. It attended their great feasts and potlatches, their council meetings and their worship services. This spirit lives on, waiting the day when material things will pass away in dust and the spirit of the people will remain.
Canoe journey, Sw̓aywi (Ambleside), 2017

—August Jack Khatsahlano, *Squamish Legends*

First Nations youth bring the canoe to the water at the Pulling Together canoe journey, Sw̓aywi (Ambleside), 2017.

Photo by John Moir

03

WEST VANCOUVER AND CAPILANO RESERVE

AN EVOLVING DIALOGUE

The Squamish Nation (Skwxwú7mesh Úxwumixw) is one of several Indigenous Nations that make up the Coast Salish Peoples. The traditional Squamish territory runs between what we now call Point Grey and Roberts Creek, north to the Elaho River headwaters, southwest to the confluence of the Soo and Green Rivers, south to Port Moody, then west back to Point Grey. Although it is all unceded land, most of the Squamish people now live in seven communities in West Vancouver, North Vancouver and within or nearby the District of Squamish. The largest of these, Capilano (Kiapilano) Reserve No. 5, sits on 1.7 square kilometres of land situated on the north shore of the inlet at the First Narrows, where drivers exit the Lions Gate Bridge into North and West Vancouver.

In 1873, a federal order-in-council to BC required eighty acres to be set aside for each Indigenous family of five, presuming that would be enough for them to pursue their traditional hunting and fishing patterns. BC countered with an offer of twenty acres. Ottawa agreed, provided it were given to every family regardless of size, to which BC agreed if the grant be given only to those not already supplied with land. Little if any consultation with the Squamish people took place. What we can now see as understandable resentment among the Squamish over the minimal extent of land allocated to reserves intensified over the next

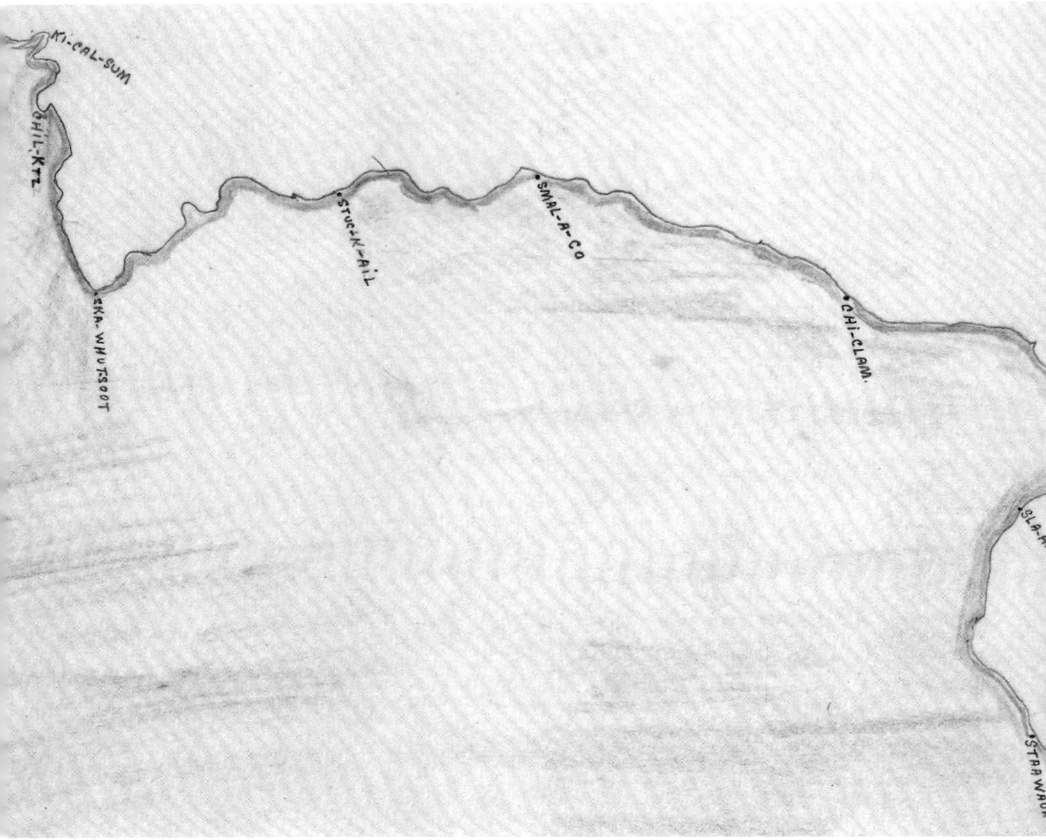

This detail from a map, drafted in 1932 by Major J.S. Matthews, shows "Indian villages and landmarks...before the white man came." From the mouth of the Capilano on the far right to Eagle Harbour area on the far left, First Nations people had occupied areas along West Vancouver's coast long before the arrival of Europeans. *City of Vancouver Archives, AM1594–: MAP 56.03*

years, with some fearing an "Indian war." To allay these tensions, in 1877 BC set up a three-man commission, which over the next thirty-five years made what they considered suitable adjustments to the BC reserves. The Squamish, quite rightly, disagreed. Title to the reserve lands remained with the province, which the Indigenous people have found far from satisfactory.[36] To this day, West Vancouver sits on unceded land.

In the latter part of the nineteenth century, the Squamish Nation came under attack from a number of quarters. Reverend Forbes and the Catholic church were incensed at the "rampant debauchery" with which "evil white men" had debased the Indigenous population. Colonel Richard Moody, whose Royal Engineers had completed a road from Vancouver to New Westminster in 1859, had a new role for his soldiers: "destroy the whole tribe." According to Forbes, this was only averted by Squamish Chief Snatt promising to convert all the Squamish people to Christianity.

There can be no doubt that the "evil white men" to whom Forbes referred continued to do harm; it's well documented. But it's equally well documented that men such as Forbes, no matter how well intentioned, inflicted a different type of harm. Only a few decades later, Forbes expressed satisfaction that "only a generation has elapsed and from an ignorant and wild tribe we find them educated and speaking the English better than they speak their own language."[37] He and others like him had no concept of the lasting negative impacts of such forced "civilization."

Chief Joe Capilano had, in the late nineteenth century, visited Indigenous communities on the Coast and Vancouver Island to talk about Native rights, especially in regard to hunting and fishing. Widely respected and a prominent figure in relatively recent Squamish history, Chief Capilano was born Mathias Joe. He took the name Joe Capilano in 1908, when he led a delegation including Cowichan Chief Charley Isipaymilt and Shuswap (Secwepemc) Chief Basil David to Ottawa and then on to England. In London, they lobbied King Edward VII for recognition of his people's land claims, emphasizing that aboriginal title had not been extinguished, and expressing concern to King Edward and Queen Alexandra about the number of incoming settlers, who often encroached on Indigenous land without permission. Although no concrete action was forthcoming from the king or his representatives, this was an important step for the Indigenous people in taking protests into their own hands. On his return, Chief Capilano expelled the Roman Catholic Church from Capilano Reserve for not supporting his trip to England and continued to lobby and organize for Indigenous rights, causing considerable consternation in the white community.[38]

The community of Homulcheson (Xwemelsch'stn) on the east bank of the Capilano River, which the Squamish Nation had strategically located long before the arrival of white explorers and settlers to keep invaders out of the inlet, became the core of Capilano Reserve. It was adjacent to West Vancouver, but its members interacted little with that community. The reserve occupies the area on the waterfront on both sides of the north end of the Lions Gate Bridge. This includes land the reserve much later

Chief Joe Capilano (front row, fifth from left) stands at the North Van ferry wharf with a group of Indigenous leaders, on his way to meet with Prime Minister Wilfred Laurier in Ottawa, 1908. *North Vancouver Museum and Archives, NVA 957. Elliott and Baglow photo*

leased to British Properties for Park Royal South. Originally 165 acres in 1870, an addition was made in 1877. On April 4, 1893, in an "Amended Minute of Decision" the reserve was redefined as 444 acres. However, the size of the reserve and its boundaries varies in different documents, making it difficult to determine if there was a definite boundary in the early years. Later, Chief Capilano indicated that the reserve was 530 acres before additional lands (later appropriately described as the "cut-off lands") were removed. The official size of the reserve is now 1.7 square kilometres, or about 420 acres. In West Vancouver's early days, settlers

considered this swampy waterfront less desirable. The land to which the Squamish were confined soon came to be considered some of the most valuable real estate in the Lower Mainland.

The governments of the day often disrespected the reserve boundaries they'd agreed to. In 1890–91, for example, the BC government permitted Alfred and Joseph Bouillon to log seventy-four acres of reserve land that ran north from Marine Drive along Capilano Road almost to the present Upper Levels Highway, then back down the east bank of the Capilano to Marine Drive. In 1893, the provincial reserve commission formally removed this land, which now includes Klahanie Park, several commercial properties and a residential subdivision, from the reserve's properties. This remains a thorn in the side of Squamish administrators over a century later. In 1988, Chief Joe Mathias, great-grandson of Chief

Chief Capilano died in 1910. His stone mausoleum still stands on a small patch of Squamish land on Sentinel Hill, in the 900 block of Keith Road. He was respected by West Vancouverites in his time. Here, two teachers from Ontario, friends of local businessman W.C. Thompson, visit his tomb in 1917. *West Vancouver Museum and Archives, 358.WVA.PHO*

Joe Capilano, voiced plans to sue the federal government, seeking either another piece of what is now called Crown land of equal value or a cash payment. As he says, "They never got the consent or received the consent of the Squamish people . . . They just stole the land."

Racism has expressed itself in different ways in West Vancouver. Discrimination against the Chinese and other Asians has often been institutionalized, with rules limiting where they could live (not in the British Properties) and work (not on the building of the Lions Gate Bridge). Although discrimination against Asians did not disappear with the removal of these rules, instances of overt racism decreased considerably.

The situation with the Squamish Nation has been different, a deeper and darker shadow that continues to cast its pall on much of the present day. They were not on the list of groups excluded from purchasing in British Properties, but few if any live or have lived there. The Indian Act of 1876 confined them to reserves, making it impossible for a highly developed hunting-and-gathering people to continue practising their way of life successfully, as they had done for millennia. The stated goal of this legislation was to assimilate them by denying them their culture. They were not allowed to retain names in their own language or speak their own language, and many of their important cultural traditions, such as the potlatch, were outlawed. Government-instituted band council elections replaced their own traditional governance structures. The act restricted them from leaving the reserve, selling produce they'd grown, or even getting married without the permission of the Indian agent. It denied them Canadian citizenship and barred them from most professions. Since 1951 revisions have eliminated its most harmful aspects, but its legacy remains.

After the Second World War, Joe and Judy Mathias (great-grandchildren of Chief Joe Capilano) became the first Squamish students to attend public school in West Vancouver, where they experienced prejudice and isolation—"a difficult lonely experience" recalls former Chief Wendy John. No Indigenous person attended UBC until a girl from Victoria enrolled in 1949.

Section 46 of the Indian Act stated that, on payment of compensation, "A municipality has power, on passing a by-law for the purpose, to expropriate land for the establishment and opening up of streets within the boundaries of the municipality." BC's population and economy were growing, and many of the railway, mining and timber companies cast hungry eyes on land they increasingly desired for their profit. In 1901, BC premier James Dunsmuir requested the (Liberal) federal government to decrease the size of the reserves.

Although this was turned down, it was open season on reserve land. The May 13, 1913, minutes from West Vancouver council include the following resolution from the city clerk of North Vancouver, asking the West Vancouver council to

> *join in the request to the Provincial Government to purchase the Indian Reserves. Moved by Counc. Gintzburger, Seconded by Coun.*

Hodges That a letter be forwarded from this council to the Provincial Government requesting the Government to purchase the Mission and Capilano Indian Reserves and that same be leased or sold by the Government at reasonable rates for industrial sites.

Richard McBride, BC premier from 1903 to 1915, collided with Prime Minister Wilfred Laurier; both argued for the right to control the apportionment of land to reserves. On September 21, 1911, when Robert Borden's Conservatives replaced Laurier, the BC government felt it had a friendlier voice in Ottawa. The McKenna-McBride Commission was formed to investigate the land question, but without any discussion of Indigenous title.[39] Dr. J. McKenna, a long-time employee of the federal department of Indian Affairs, was the federal representative. From 1913 to 1916, the five-man group travelled through BC, gathering information that was used to readjust the boundaries of many reserves. McKenna stated that "if we should recommend that a portion of this reserve should be cut off, it could not be done unless you Indians here consent to it being done.…We told them that if the Indians needed more land they would get it." The commission did not follow its own stated rules, deciding that it would recommend cut-offs and let the federal government deal with obtaining consent. In 1919, the federal government introduced legislation extinguishing that need. As one Indigenous commentator later said, "It's like changing the rules so you can't win after the lacrosse game is over."

The white population was generally unsympathetic. On June 19, 1913, at hearings being held by the Royal Commission on Indian Affairs, Reeve May of the District of North Vancouver called the Mission Indian Reserve in North Vancouver (just to the east of the Capilano Reserve) "a block to progress and it was the wish of the people as a whole that the obstruction should be removed.…The Indians have done nothing to improve their land and the price of the land has gone up by leaps and bounds by the improvements that have been effected by the white people of the North Shore."

Squamish Chief Joseph objected. "Until we get a clear title to this land no proposition from anyone will be entertained." In a 1913 letter signed by Squamish activist Andy Paull and the missionary Reverend C.M. Tate, the authors warned that "the commissioners were 'political friends of the provincial government,' which historically claimed Indians had no rights in BC." At this time, PGE was in the process of acquiring 11.89 acres of

Squamish land for railway purposes, as the line they would open in 1914 cut through the reserve.

The commission recommended cut-offs on thirty-five reserves, all but one of which (Capilano Reserve) were outside Metro Vancouver. The cut-offs severed 36,000 acres from reserves and added 87,010 acres. Although that sounds generous, the severed land was valued at $1.4 million and the added land at $400,000. The extremely valuable Capilano Reserve cut-off land ran along the waterfront from the current duck pond to 400 metres east of the Lions Gate Bridge. This land could be subdivided and sold by the province with the consent of the federal government's Department of Indian Affairs, with half of the proceeds going to the reserve and half to the federal government "for the use and benefit of the Indians" but not under the control of the Squamish people. This land remained lost to the Squamish's Capilano Reserve for the next seventy years.

The Capilano River and the adjacent foreshore were a prime source for the Navvy Jack gravel highly valued for construction in Vancouver. On April 13, 1913, "the band hereby consents to a license to dredge and remove sand and gravel on the part above mentioned of the fore-shore opposite the reserve being granted to the said James Stewart."[40] Following the First World War, they made other concessions. On February 7, 1920, an agreement was reached to dredge "an approximate area of 45 acres and being composed of the bed of the Capilano River within the limits of the said reserve."[41]

In 1916, Indigenous people from many nations formed the Allied Tribes of BC to protect land claims. In 1926, they made their final claim to the federal government before the hammer came down. A joint Senate-House committee, which had been created to hear their land claims, recommended a $100,000 annual grant for economic and social improvement of BC Indians. But it also made it a criminal offense for Indian organizations to raise funds to seek a land claim settlement. This draconian law remained in place until the late 1940s.

Fighting for Control

In the meantime, on July 23, 1923, after eight years of discussion and planning, sixteen Squamish-speaking tribes signed a legal document to form one nation. This document declared that the traditional governance of the Squamish was still in place, as was their traditional life. Simon Baker, who served as a councillor for the Squamish Nation for thirty years, ten of these as chief, recalled clams being a main food source. The people often travelled by canoe across what is now called the First Narrows, where they sold berries, clams and eggs. They took logs to Hastings Mill for milling, in return for which they got half the lumber, which was used to build the early houses on the Capilano Reserve. But disease and poor living conditions decimated the band. By 1931, only seventeen families, mostly interrelated, lived on the Capilano Reserve.

As West Vancouver grew, its development eroded reserve land, reducing the already small area to which the Squamish had been confined. The PGE took over parts of the severed land for their right-of-way and land for the north end of the Lions Gate Bridge was expropriated. Another 0.91 acres as a residence for the lighthouse keeper was removed by the federal Department of Marine and Fisheries, with 1.63 acres added to that in 1947. On October 24, 1946, a letter from H.E. Taylor, Indian agent, discussed the leasing of a portion of the reserve for a gravel crushing plant. Although he explored what he considered to be all the conceivable objections to the lease, concluding that "the only justification for withholding a permit would be possible danger to the First Narrows Bridge structure," nowhere did he mention Indigenous title. In 1954 nine acres from the reserve were allocated as a possible site from which to build another bridge across the inlet. And so the reserve was progressively carved away.

A number of ensuing plans proposed even more uses for reserve land. The 1945 West Vancouver Town Planning Commission Report stated that "on both sides of the Capilano River, large portions of the Capilano Indian Reserve are recommended for acquisition for park purposes."[42] With the improved access provided by the Lions Gate Bridge, West Vancouver was growing rapidly (although so was the Indigenous population), increasing the reserve land's value. Some West Vancouverites expressed indignation at gravel-removing leases on the reserve, fearing that industrial projects would increase, as the 1926 bylaw left open. In 1948, BPP unsuccessfully bid on the purchase of sixty-five acres of reserve land to create a park as a showpiece entrance to their development. Some non-Indigenous people objected to what they considered the rough appearance of the Indigenous residential community below the Lions Gate Bridge, which they may have found incompatible with the middle-class cleanliness and order promoted by the municipality.

In 1950, the Metropolitan Park Planning Committee pushed to acquire waterfront reserve land to use as a park, which came close to spelling the reserve's end. The committee sent an offer to the Department of Lands in Victoria, to be forwarded to Ottawa, to purchase the entire reserve plus the cut-off lands for $60,000. The offer included a certified cheque. Where the reserve's original inhabitants would live was a little hazy, although there was some talk of building a subdivision on the reserve to accommodate them. There is no evidence the federal government responded.

The desirability of this land only increased as the years went by. By 1952 there had been thirty-eight offers to purchase portions of the reserve land west of the Lions Gate Bridge. Meanwhile there was insufficient housing for the reserve's residents. By the mid-'50s the reserve population had increased, but only slightly, to 182. Substantial increases would take place in ensuing years, giving the Squamish a greater presence and power.

Decisions on alienation of land for leases were made by a majority vote of the population of the Squamish Nation with advice from the Indian superintendent and the Indian commissioner. Practically, however, if they refused to lease their lands for such projects as the PGE right-of-way or the north end of the Lions Gate Bridge, the land would have been taken anyway. A 1956 municipal report described "vast undeveloped acreage" on the reserve. At this time most of the Squamish people were located in the northeast portion of the reserve east of Capilano River between Marine Drive and Welch Street. The report considered this area "more than adequate" for their population.

Under this plan, the municipality intended to use most of the reserve land west of Capilano River for a municipal park. The northwest section (roughly where Park Royal South would be) would become a home to service and light industrial uses such as gas stations, lumberyards, sheet metal shops and warehouses. From the Capilano River to the Lions Gate Bridge was designated for unspecified provincial purposes, and from Lions Gate Bridge east for gravel extraction and restricted industrial use. The report stated that because most of the reserve land was flat and low-lying, it was more suited to industrial than residential use. The so-called Indian village would screen the new North Vancouver development of Norgate from the industrial area; it was apparently not thought to be a problem for the Squamish residents to look out their windows at industry. An area east of Capilano River was considered for a municipal recreation area, possibly including a stadium, ballpark, ornamental gardens and a swimming pool. These plans did not materialize.

As noted, throughout the first part of the last century, many of the Indigenous people and their supporters fought vigorously for fair and equal treatment. Chief Simon Baker, also known as Khot-la-Cha or "kind heart," was a strong voice for the Squamish people throughout his thirty years as a councillor, including ten as chief, from roughly the 1940s to the 1960s. He worked tirelessly to empower his people. In the 1940s he founded the Coqualeetza Fellowship Club, a precursor to the Northwest Indian Cultural Society, and also established the First Nations House of Learning at UBC and the Vancouver Aboriginal Friendship Centre. In addition to receiving such honours as the BC Centennial Award of Merit (twice), Order of Canada, National Aboriginal Achievement Award for Heritage and Spirituality, honorary graduate of the Native Indian Teacher Education Program, and honorary Doctor of Laws at UBC, he was the only Squamish member ever designated Chief for Lifetime. Verna Kirkness, who authored his biography, *Khot-la-Cha*, wrote, "He kept his culture alive when most weren't worrying about it too much." In the book, Baker recounts one of the steps toward taking back control. He

A powerful cultural advocate for the Squamish and Pacific Northwest First Nations, Chief Simon Baker (Khot-la-Cha) is pictured in 1960. *VPL.44654, photo Eric Cable*

> *recalls how in the 1940s Band meetings were chaired and controlled by the Indian Agent, also the Treasurer, who withheld financial information. "The Indian Agent always said that what I was asking for would take money. I knew we had money from the sale of land and gravel. Fifty per cent went to distribution, twenty-five dollars per person, which was given to us at Christmas time; the other fifty per cent went into our capital account.*
>
> *"I asked Mr. Ball, the Indian Agent, how much money we had in our capital fund, when we could get it and what we could use it for. He said, 'Well, I don't know, but whatever you take out will affect your*

distribution.' So I said to him, 'I get twenty-five dollars, my wife gets twenty-five dollars, and the next day we're broke and many of our people still don't have no running water, no lights.'

"Finally he told us that we had $800,000, but if we took it out we'd lose our distribution. I told him it would help our people much more if we all had sewers, water and electricity. . . we decided to ask for half of our money, $400,000. Just at that time they were getting rid of wartime houses. . . . We figured out how many houses we could get from our money, including the sewer and water. So we got so many houses. They wanted us to have a boulevard. To build a boulevard would have cost us $500,000. . . . I said to the council, 'Let's get rid of this guy. We don't need him. Let's do it ourselves.'"[43]

Mr. Anfield was the next Indian agent. When he resigned in 1965, Baker replaced him.

Gaining Momentum

The most important lease was in 1960 of sixty-seven acres of the northwest part of the reserve land for the initial development of Park Royal South. The British Properties expressed interest in using its Park Royal lease as a launching pad for other enterprises. On August 29, 1967, BPP manager Peter Finch wrote to municipal manager E.G. Barnes, "I should like to confirm my interest in the possibility of this company establishing an industrial estate on land east of the Lions Gate Bridge." Later he expressed a wish that "the expansion of the Park Royal area can take place as a comprehensive development including the Shopping Centre itself."

From the municipality's perspective, they faced a difficult problem: the Capilano Reserve is geographically contiguous with District of West Vancouver land and shares many of the same concerns. It is at the front door of a community that historically has prided itself on elegance and sophistication. However, as the Squamish people had by this time suffered countless assaults and abuses, poverty and disease in the name of assimilation, it's not surprising that they had little sympathy for the preoccupations of their neighbours. Yet the vagaries of history left them with no choice but to interact with the urban community they found themselves surrounded by, and make continual efforts to assert their rights.

In the late 1960s, the Squamish people continued their tireless efforts to take back economic and political control of their land and their destiny.

In 1967, Dan Baker opened the seventy-four unit Capilano Trailer Park beneath the Lions Gate Bridge with a government loan of $25,000, the first of any size to an Indigenous person; the reserve received 10 per cent of the gross revenue. His son Frank took it over in 1976. A 1968 plan for the Nahanie Hotel on the waterfront below the PGE at the east end of Ambleside Park did not go ahead, but sent ripples of consternation through the West Vancouver community.

In the same year, the band council took over negotiating land deals from the district superintendent of Indian Affairs. Band constable Ted Steward commented, "You can't buy Indians off with a bottle of rum and a ten dollar bill anymore." One of the ways the Squamish have demonstrated this has been by becoming increasingly successful in the real estate game.

Tough battles remained to be won, as the "Indian village" was sequestered in 48.4 acres in the northeast part of the reserve, with much of the rest of the reserve alienated by short- and long-term leases. A 1968 report by Acres Western Limited painted a dismal picture of a population mired in poverty, declining in numbers. In 1964 the average per capita income of Indigenous people on the North Shore was $630, compared with a BC average of $2,579. The underlying assumption was that, as the Indigenous people faded away, 265 acres of the reserve would become "available for development." The addition of ten thousand residents (certainly not Indigenous) on 101.6 acres in the next fifteen years was envisaged. A high density of twenty to eighty units per acre was proposed, which would certainly be a windfall for any developer if implemented (which it wasn't).

The report reflects the paternalistic attitudes of the times, and indicates no appreciation of Indigenous culture. They were considered no more than children to be instructed. "To ensure that all members are familiar with the financial capability and limitation of themselves, and of the Band, short courses, technical assistance, and pilot projects on using money are suggested."[44]

In 1969, then minister of Indian and Northern Affairs Jean Chrétien wrote to the provincial government that the Squamish band had "a moral if not legal claim to the unused portion of the cut-off lands." He later stated, "They were given some land and the land was cut off without the consent of the Indians. I wanted to tell the British Columbia government that some of the land in B.C. had been cut off and the provincial government should return the land to the Indians because it was cut off without their consent." Negotiations between federal and provincial representatives led to an offer in 1973 by provincial Minister of Lands Ray Williston to return half of the lands severed. The Squamish people rejected the offer.

At this time, big developments had become common; major real estate transactions were in the air and occasionally on the ground. In 1971 a report titled "Development Concept for I.R. 5 and D.L. 5521," sponsored by the Squamish Nation and the three North Shore municipal councils and mostly concerning land east of the Capilano River, produced some grandiose visions that would have permanently changed the reserve. The report proposed movie theatres, motels, hotels and restaurants for the northern part of the reserve, with a million square feet of office space projected for an area north of the PGE right-of-way. Retail and service stores, an "Indian" trade centre and numerous apartment buildings would provide accommodation for up to 20,000 people. The consortium retained internationally renowned architect Moshe Safde. This project would provide employment for 1,200 band members for twenty-five years, an attractive proposition when half of the band was unemployed. Although the International Plaza Hotel, now an apartment building, opened in 1971, other aspects of the project did not materialize at that time, although other plans are always on the back burner.

In 1970, a court case between the District of Surrey and Peace Arch Enterprises Ltd. confirmed that Indigenous people controlled zoning on reserve land. So did this mean that West Vancouver had no control over the zoning of I.R. 5? That did indeed appear to be the case. The municipal government was more than a little unhappy at that prospect; West Vancouver's mayor Peter Jones threatened to appeal the Peace Arch decision to the Supreme Court. Later, mayor Don Lanskail said, "we are going to have to scream to Ottawa to get control of these lands." Band council chairman David Jacobs bluntly replied, "you do not seem willing to accept us as a neighbouring municipality or community with a separate jurisdiction from your own. You want us to give up control of our land to your municipality and make everything we do with our land subject to your prior approval."

As disadvantaged citizens of countries as diverse as El Salvador, Zimbabwe and China have learned, land reform is an essential component of significant social change. Generally this involves disadvantaged groups wresting control of the land away from the government or major landowners. Across Canada, First Nations are engaged in an ongoing struggle to have their title to the land formally recognized and to regain control over land the federal and provincial governments have controlled, despite the fact that the land has often never been ceded (as is the case for the Squamish people). The Squamish Nation's drive to manage their reserve land, at the very least, takes place in this context.

Chief Joe Mathias was one of the main leaders in the fight for a better deal for his people. From 1969 until his death in 2000, he was political spokesman for the Squamish Nation, respected by all for his quiet intelligence and dedication, working to implement treaty rights and land claims. "We have been part of the growth of Vancouver for decades and now we want to share in that growth. The original occupants have been isolated from economic and financial development." Peter Jones, who became mayor in 1974, initially attempted a conciliatory approach. In 1972, he wrote that "the greatest challenge facing West Vancouver is to achieve co-operation between both Indian and non-Indian people so that the ultimate development of the truly unique Indian lands would be a habitat of outstanding merit, satisfying the cultural and economic needs of the Squamish Indian Band and being a source of joy and pride to all." But given that a 1971 municipal report suggested extending Ambleside Park to include reserve land on the east side of the Capilano River, not all members of the municipality were on board.

The Squamish Indian Band Capilano Reserve No. 5 Urban Design Study (1976) struck a vastly different note from the earlier paternalistic report by Acres. This report expressed their wishes. In the introduction to the later report, the band council stated that "we can no longer remain docile and dormant and watch other municipalities take advantage of this growth." The study had been initiated in 1973; over the next few years, band members were involved at every step of the way in establishing a political framework for their future. In one of the mantras of the day, they "participated in the process rather than confronting results." The report frankly assessed the problems of their land, split east and west by the Lions Gate Bridge and north and south by the BC Railway, with numerous short- and long-term leases cutting up the land while ignoring its natural attributes. But it was clearly their land. Although they did not develop most of the major plans proposed, the report made it clear that the Squamish people were now the ones calling the shots.

In 1975, the BC government responded by acknowledging the improper way in which the McKenna-McBride Commission had reduced the acreage of twenty-two reserves seventy years earlier. The BC government then established a Commission of Inquiry to examine the nature and extent of each reduction, and on June 25, 1975, the province, municipality and Indigenous peoples met in the first official negotiations. After that committee dissolved in 1981, discussion with the province proceeded on a reserve-by-reserve basis, with the federal government generally encouraging the more reluctant provincial government to reach a settlement.

West Vancouver municipality had little formal clout, but frequently expressed concern over issues that affected it. On August 8, 1975, Mayor Jones wrote band leader David Jacobs expressing concern over what he felt was the lack of an overall plan by the Squamish. "The exclusion of one class of land, Indian land, from the general zoning control of land within the municipality is a source of potential frustration, and can lead to disorderly development. Because of this we believe that, wherever Indian land lies within a Municipality, region or province, it is in the interest of both the Band and the government to have the anomaly corrected." He called for "Open, constructive and meaningful discussions and action," stating in a February 19, 1976, memo to council that "we should not allow any development to start without providing for an effective West Vancouver voice in controlled future stages in development of this land." Part of the context of this was the expansion plans for Park Royal South on Squamish land, over which the municipality wished to have more control.

Jacobs's response to Jones emphasized, "Our Band is the authority for determining the use of land on our reserves," and the Squamish supported this sentiment both through formal negotiations and public protests. In June 1975, over three hundred members of the reserve picketed the highways development works yard and a private gravel yard, both of which were on reserve property. This and other protests helped accelerate government responses.

Heritage Reclaimed

> We walk into the future backwards because we are looking to our ancestors. If you are listening to our ancestors you are learning our traditions and culture. What was given to you is now in your arms. So that sometime in the future you can turn around and give it to your grandchildren. What took place you can give to your children. That is the value of our circle.
>
> —Chief Joe Mathias

Although many disagreements remain ongoing, in this instance the Squamish Nation's work paid off. The federal and provincial governments approved the return of the cut-off lands (116 acres) in 1983. This included 25.9 acres of verdant Ambleside Park south of the PGE tracks between the waterfowl refuge and Capilano River, then worth over $11 million (much more now). This had come none too soon for the Squamish. There had been twelve major development schemes advanced for Ambleside Park in the thirteen years prior to 1979, including some that wanted to make it the Stanley Park of the North Shore.

The repatriated section of Ambleside Park included the pitch-and-putt golf course, the fitness track, dog run and Seawalk. The reserve also received $1.5 million for land that could not be returned (especially land used by the north end of the Lions Gate Bridge and the PGE right-of-way), and $115,000 annually for at least five years as rent for the municipal works yard and sewage treatment plant, which were on their land. The agreement to return the land was finally ratified by Privy Council Order 235 on February 23, 1989.

Many local politicians and non-Indigenous residents maintained their opposition to the return of the cut-off lands, fearing non-Indigenous use of Ambleside Park would be affected. Tension between the community and the reserve continued. Mayor Derrick Humphreys channelled the resentment of many West Vancouverites, who felt that their development of this swampland into a beautiful park gave them some rights: "The land was waste land and has been converted into a high-cost pitch-and-putt golf course, and an attractive natural habitat of duck lagoon, an extension of the harbor sea-wall, an extensive exercise circuit and a canine exercise area." In the view of the Squamish people, however, what

West Vancouver spent on their land was none of their concern, especially when they knew they might not retain possession. Some might very well have preferred it to have been left in its natural state, with lagoons and marshy areas in which to canoe and gather plants, fish and shoot ducks to sustain their traditional lifestyle. The Squamish had (and still have) made a point of keeping their options open, including building commercial properties on the waterfront, while making it clear that they have no immediate plans to exclude West Vancouverites from the use of this land. But their point is well made. As Chief Joe Mathias said, "Now you know how my grandfather, my grandmother and all our people felt. Now you know how it felt to us to have our land stolen."

West Vancouver's provision of services such as police, water and fire protection to the reserve served as the municipality's main lever in negotiations. Some municipal representatives initially wanted the pipes providing services to be sized only to serve the proposed development on the reserve, not the ultimate development. In this way, perhaps, the municipality felt it could limit growth. On the other hand, Mathias argued that, as they now owned Ambleside Park, the public should be required to pay for its use.

In 1986, the municipality offered $20,000 a year for its rent of Ambleside Park, a substantial increase over the pittance of $3,206 paid by the provincial government to West Vancouver since 1957 (only half of which went to the Squamish Nation), but well below market value. The band insisted on a heftier increase to $50,000 to which the municipality reluctantly agreed for a two-year term commencing February 1, 1986. A 1994 Interim Services Agreement set out terms for providing services to the Squamish lands by the district, specifying the remuneration the district would receive.

In 1974 Ottawa signed a seventy-one-year lease agreement with the Squamish Nation for fifty-five acres just east of the Lions Gate Bridge to build a 400,000-square-foot environment centre for their western operations. Over a thousand people were to be employed here. The rent, initially $241,000 a year, was to be adjusted every five years based on revised appraisals of the land. Because of budget cuts, the federal government cancelled their plans for this project in 1976. The Squamish Nation insisted that any use of the land should be as an environment centre, or at least have some environmental relationship, as had been planned at the time they negotiated the lease. Land being the valuable commodity it is in West Vancouver, by 1995 the federal government was paying $4.4 million a year to the Squamish for land with which they were doing nothing. In the fall of 1999 Chief Mathias finally negotiated a land-use plan with the Department of Environment that included a resolution of this issue.

The long struggle for the Squamish Nation and other Indigenous peoples to have their land title recognized continues. Except for a few communities on Vancouver Island and in the northeast of the province, most BC nations have not signed treaties and the provincial government has been in no hurry to do so. Chief Mathias criticized the province's lack of recognition of land claims, although since 1990 negotiations have been proceeding, if slowly. In 1992, the Squamish banded together with thirty-two other BC First Nations to file notice of intent to participate in negotiating treaties through the BC Treaty Commission, with Mathias the first official land claims coordinator. The Squamish Nation focused on land and water use, compensation, resource development and creating a structure for a relationship between the land and neighbouring communities. Chief Mathias stated that the goal of the treaty process was "self-governing authority over land, resources, education, health, social services, taxation and infrastructure."[45] Currently they are at stage three of a six-stage process, in which the goal is to negotiate a framework agreement, identify the subjects and objectives of the negotiations, and establish a timetable and procedural arrangements. However, they have been stalled at this stage since 1996. On Mathias's death in 2000, Chief Gibby Jacob took over his role and responsibilities.

A persistent issue for the Squamish Nation has been raising funds to provide services its members need—the type of amenities a municipality would provide. In 1988, amendments to the Indian Act gave reserves the power to pass bylaws related to designated lands (leased lands within a reserve). In 1992, the Squamish initiated plans to collect property taxes from the leased lands to provide community facilities and other services.

The population of the reserve continues to grow much faster than the housing supply. Since the 1970s, only fifteen houses a year have been built, although eight hundred people are on the housing wait list. The 2016 census identified the reserve population as 2,931, a healthy increase from 2,700 in 2011. Only about a third of these are Indigenous, and with the projected apartment developments it's likely that the proportion of non-Indigenous residents of Squamish lands will increase.

The Capilano Master Plan Summary, December 2004, lays out future plans. Community use, centred in the northeast and on the east bank of the Capilano River below the railway, will occupy 45 per cent of the land. This will include approximately 180 single-family homes and 300 multi-family homes. Economic development will occupy 39.5 per cent of the land, including high-rise apartment buildings, low-rise apartment/condominium complexes and townhomes—no industry and minimal commercial development. A large development at Marine Drive and Taylor Way will include a high-rise, with twelve spaces for supported living and six short-term housing units. The remaining 15.5 per cent is designated as an environmental preserve to provide protection for sensitive areas and recreational space. The First Nations Certainty of Land Act, passed in 2009, harmonized provincial legislation on federally administered reserve lands, spurring talk of $7 billion worth of development and more than 15,000 jobs.

Making plans reality has been slow. On December 1, 2016, David Negrin, the president of Aquilini Development and Construction Inc., was named the CEO of the MST Development Corp., which manages the billions of dollars of land owned by the Musqueam, Squamish and Tsleil Waututh. Total self-government in a democratic framework is a clear goal, and they are moving steadily in that direction. Chief Joe Mathias was one of the first to look forward to a new system, decrying the failure of that created by the federal government. It's "failed in housing, it's failed in social development, it's failed in education and in terms of our economic well-being. That's why we want the fundamental human right to govern ourselves."[46]

Different cultures express themselves and their values differently. Where much of West Vancouver expresses itself through architecture, the culture of the Squamish and other Indigenous people expresses itself in other ways. One of these is canoe races. Canoe journeys are an apt cultural symbol; races express unity, harmony—working together to get somewhere. As cultural adviser Maurice Nahanee states, "a large part of the journey is from within, to become a better person." The Ambleside war canoe races were revived in July 1988, attracting paddlers from Indigenous groups from the Lower Mainland, Washington state and Vancouver Island. In 1992 Cedric Billy carved the first ocean-going canoe in fifty years. At its launch on August 27, band manager Glen Newman described the spirit it fostered as "a value system in which

A seagoing canoe leaves Sw̓aywi (Ambleside), during the Pulling Together Canoe Journey, 2017. *Photo by John Moir*

each member of a community is cared about, from the youngest child to the most honored elder."[47] Since 2001, First Nations along with West Vancouver Police and other groups have been taking part in the annual Pulling Together canoe journey that blends together culture, Indigenous spirituality and teamwork. Nahanee describes the community nature of this event as "an essential and defining quality of Pacific Northwest Indigenous people."

Language is an essential way every culture expresses itself. Although the Squamish language (Skwxwú7mesh sníchim) had been declared extinct in 1930, a number of elders retained fluency. In 1967 a Dutch linguist, Aert Kuipers, published a four-hundred-page dictionary and grammar of the Squamish language. The same year, Squamish Elder Chief Louis Miranda, who received an honorary doctorate from Simon Fraser University in 1981, began research with several UBC professors on the language, subsequently developing a writing system. Chief Simon Baker, who promoted education as a key to a better life by providing the tools necessary for self-determination, also received an honorary doctorate (from UBC) in 1990. After Indigenous students were integrated into the North Vancouver school system in 1969, classes in the Squamish language were started at St. Thomas Aquinas High School in 1972, with *The Curriculum for Squamish as a Second Language* produced in 1985. A Squamish-English dictionary was completed in 2011, and in 2014 a Squamish language program was made available at Capilano University.

Chief Lawrence Baker has said, "My biggest concern is to make people

Victor Harry holds the Squamish Nation staff during the Grand Entry at the Capilano Pow Wow, 2017. *Photo by John Moir*

The Grand Entry at the annual Capilano Pow Wow. This celebration of Indigenous culture has been an annual event for over thirty years, bringing together Native groups from across Western Canada and the United States. *Photo by John Moir*

At the Department of Fisheries Research Station open house in West Vancouver in 2017, Squamish and Tsleil Waututh acknowledge cooperation with a welcoming address and song. From left to right: Squamish delegation Leanne Lewis, Randall Lewis, Councillor Chris Lewis and Tsleil Waututh Chief Maureen Thomas. *Photo by John Moir*

Sea-going canoes traverse Burrard Inlet, establishing a presence in the waters of their ancestors. It is an action that will be repeated many times, as the local First Nations communities demand consultation on the use and preservation of these waters.
Photo by John Moir

aware that the culture and the language is on the edge of extinction." In 1988, 150 Indigenous children were acquiring a greater awareness of their place in the world through studying their language and culture at a number of North Vancouver schools, as well as a nursery school located on the reserve. But reviving a language that another culture has worked hard to extinguish is not easy. In 2011 only ten fluent speakers of Squamish remained, although efforts continue to expand this base.

Although it remains an ongoing battle, the Squamish people are successfully asserting the importance and value of their culture; that said, the next steps are unclear. As noted, negotiations for their land claims have been at a standstill for many years, and indeed many Indigenous people are deeply skeptical of the negotiation process, some calling it the "ultimate colonial economic manipulation." One way or another, the process may introduce new dimensions to the lives of all West Vancouverites and reshape the connections they have with their neighbours.

> "This seems to be the place to be."
>
> —Queen Elizabeth (the Queen Mother) on her 1939 visit.

This 1930s Olmsted sketch for a "First Narrows Bridge" emphasizes stateliness and symmetry, with vaguely sketched but grand statuary at the entrance. No lions as yet.

Courtesy of the National Park Service, Frederick Law Olmsted National Historic Site

04

BRITISH PACIFIC PROPERTIES

BUILD IT AND THEY WILL (EVENTUALLY) COME

The Vision

Queen Elizabeth has continued hanging her chapeau in Buckingham Palace, but many notables have found residence in the British Pacific Properties a congenial fit. In the 1980s the Aga Khan maintained an occasional home, and many others, some famous and most affluent, have enjoyed the lifestyle that living here affords. Douglas Coupland and Sarah McLachlan are two of the many artists who live or have lived here, as well as billionaire business mogul Jim Pattison. Visiting film stars such as Matt Damon have enjoyed temporary residence in homes that rent for as much as $50,000 a month while doing local shoots.

Harvey Haddon from Nottingham, the first builder on the scene, had made a fortune from investing twenty thousand pounds to purchase lots at the northeast corner of Granville and Hastings and the northwest corner of Cambie and Hastings in Vancouver. In 1891 he used his substantial profits to acquire 160 acres on the North Shore, where he built his two-storey, sixteen-room mansion where the clubhouse of the Capilano Golf Course now stands. Designed by Sydney Eveleigh, his palatial residence was complemented by lily ponds, rock gardens and five hundred rose bushes imported from France, and it was staffed by Chinese servants whose quarters were in the vicinity of the 15th tee of the present Capilano Golf Course. Unfortunately, his English wife was not so enamoured with her wilderness estate, and with their son and daughter, she declined his offer of a woodland retreat in what were then the hinterlands of the North Shore. So ended Haddon's dream.

In 1926 E.P. "Pat" Burns of Burns meat packers in Alberta came close to acquiring Haddon's property, on which he proposed movie studios, a residential subdivision and a golf course. But when it came to signing the deal, Burns refused—perhaps, as West Vancouver municipal solicitor Gordon Robson said, because he was advised he was too old to undertake such an ambitious project. The property reverted to the municipality for taxes, and Haddon's mansion burned down in 1930 when a party of skiers lost control of a fire they'd lit in the middle of the main floor.

In 1926 West Vancouver's municipal clerk James Ollason realized the municipality was sitting on a large amount of property acquired through tax sales. He attempted (unsuccessfully) to persuade eastern Canadian interests to take a large part of this land in return for constructing a bridge to Vancouver. North Shore federal cabinet minister H.H. Stevens and a few of his friends took over title to a large parcel of tax sale land in 1927 for $12,500 (probably the same land), but after the 1929 crash and the death of Stevens's main financial backer, they were glad when Canadian entrepreneur Arthur James Towie Taylor came along with his plans.

A.J.T. Taylor, an energetic visionary, saw the possibilities for realizing his dreams in the mesmerizing lands at the base of the North Shore mountains. As a fourteen-year-old, he left school in Victoria when his father died, and went to work for a foundry in Nanaimo before becoming an engineering apprentice in Vancouver Shipyards and then helping to build the IOCO refinery for Imperial Oil in 1913. After surviving financial setbacks he moved to England, where he became managing director of the Underfeed Stoker Company and was accepted (for a time) as an equal in the company of the British power brokers. His promotion of BC found sympathetic ears among the remarkable Guinness family, who had risen to the pinnacle of British aristocratic eminence on their enormous profits from a working man's drink and were always on the lookout for safe havens for their money.

The Irish brewing company had been founded in 1725 by the energetic Arthur Guinness, who fathered twenty-one children and created the largest single business in Ireland. Only eight of his progeny survived childhood, but their offspring generated numerous lines of the family that spread throughout the English-speaking world; their mini-diaspora is meticulously documented in Frederic Mulally's *The Silver Salver: The Story of the Guinness Family*. Rupert Guinness visited Vancouver in 1917 on a recruiting mission for the Royal Navy Volunteers Reserve, and again in 1949. He continued to invest in Canada, including the Park Royal Shopping Centre. The Guinnesses engaged aggressively in acquisitions both at home and overseas. They feared, not without reason, that a British Labour government might limit annual income and introduce high taxation; investments abroad in trusts set up by the family were exempt from crushing British inheritance taxes. In the early twentieth century, their properties included "a Manhattan office building, an hotel in San Francisco, a Canadian oilfield, an African mine, a sheep farm in New Zealand."[48]

From 1907 to 1913, a land boom in the Lower Mainland had sent prices soaring, making today's increases, from a percentage point of view at least, seem paltry. The owner of 3.62 acres of the southeast section of D.L. 554 in West Vancouver, which runs from 22nd to 24th Street and from the waterfront back to Ottawa Avenue, sold the land for $724, then bought it back for $9,500 before selling it again for $20,000. This and similar increases were unsustainable. The depression of 1913 led to the market's collapse, and much of West Vancouver's land reverted to the municipality when the owners could no longer pay taxes. The municipality, realizing the value of this land, kept it for future possibilities.

Taylor established British Pacific Securities in 1928 to facilitate investment in BC, and enticed British investors W.S. Eyre and Lord Southborough to consider providing the necessary financial backing to develop the North Shore lands. In 1930 Taylor and Eyre made a trip to West Vancouver; Eyre was encouraged by what he saw. On a second trip in 1931, Guinness representatives Lord Southborough and Mr. Eyre accompanied Taylor, along with Mr. Greenwood, a lawyer, and C.H. Bland, financial adviser and trustee of the Iveagh trust. Joseph Leyland, who had been elected reeve in 1930, was their genial host. Their visit to West Vancouver meshed with Leyland's dream to make West Vancouver a residential community *par excellence*. Leyland had always recognized the necessity of outside capital to provide the development that would attract a larger population. And here were people of wealth and social standing far beyond that of his own English family, but with whom he could deal as equals.

On May 27, 1931, Leyland took his visitors for a tour of the property on the mountain slopes of West Vancouver. He wrote, "I felt like Moses. It was a day sent from heaven. Spring was everywhere, the air was warm and free from mist or fog." His visitors were amenable to visions of a promised land, although it would be some years before Jewish people would be allowed the privilege of residence. One of its attractions was that it was relatively high up the mountain—"Above the fog and below the snow," as it was later advertised. Many felt that this was a healthier location, away from the swampy, supposedly disease-infested waterfront. And then there was the marvellous southern exposure looking over Vancouver, rare in a land where the mountain ranges run north–south. And, potentially at least, access to downtown Vancouver was convenient. They struck a deal.

This sale came at an opportune time for West Vancouver, as the Depression had led it, like most BC communities, to the brink of bankruptcy. Tax collection, which had been 87 per cent in 1925, fell to 58 per cent in 1933, although as a result tax sales helped the city add to

In an effort to encourage sales in the late 1930s and early '40s, visitors were brought to the airy upper reaches of the "Properties" to view the panorama of Vancouver below. *City of Vancouver Archives, CVA 1376–715*

their stock of land at minimal cost. Leyland and other municipal leaders considered it unwise to sell small parcels of these tax sale lands, believing that they would only revert again to the municipality for taxes. This decision was fortuitous in enabling the municipality's acquisition of an extensive contiguous block of property.

British Pacific Properties, incorporated in the province of BC on October 8, 1931, purchased four thousand acres from the municipality, stretching from Capilano River to Horseshoe Bay between the 500- and 1,500-foot (150–454-metre) levels. This original investment was led by three Guinness brothers: Edward, the Earl of Iveagh, the Hon. A.E. Guinness and Walter, the first Baron Moyne. Ownership of the land was not complete—some other landholders held property within the geographic boundaries of the BPP's holdings—but in effect the British Properties controlled the destiny of this area. On November 18 the ratepayers of West Vancouver did not hesitate to resoundingly approve this agreement 1,329 to 26; with a payment of $28,632 in 1932, the British Properties snatched West Vancouver from the jaws of bankruptcy. BPP also bought Vancouver's Marine Building out of bankruptcy, along with surrounding land, and set up their offices on its top floor, with Taylor building a plush penthouse for his accommodation. He became the first president of BPP.

But when Leyland and his colleagues checked the acreage, there was a surprise: the four thousand acres turned out to be considerably less. Leyland recounts that "as negotiations went forward the council got a shock. In adding up the parcels we found we only had 3,000 acres. I went to Victoria, said nothing of the plan in hand, and bought 1,000 acres of Crown land for $3.75 an acre. We were, in effect, buying the 1,000 acres with money from their deposit." They then resold this land to BPP for $18.75 an acre, making a tidy profit. The municipality levied a fixed assessment of $100,000 a year on the land acquisition for the first five years, with taxes to be paid subsequently according to its valuation. The initial British Properties development focused on 1,100 acres on the easternmost part of the property, providing steady employment for one hundred men, mostly from West Vancouver.

The parallels between the British Properties and Ebenezer Howard's garden city may be coincidental but are intriguing. Howard proposed that, for his garden city, six thousand acres should be purchased for £240,000, with the central part planned as a thousand-acre development,

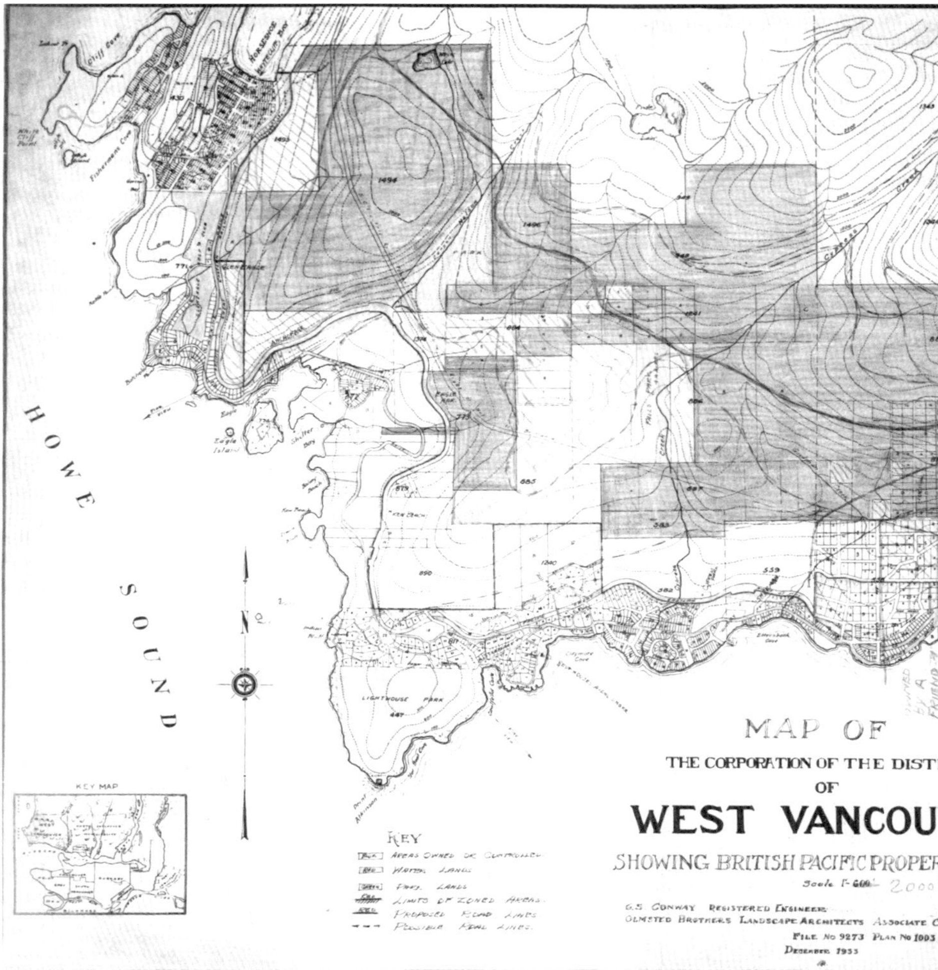

On a 1933 West Vancouver map, the Olmsted brothers sketched the British Properties lands and proposed roads, including upper level roads spanning West Vancouver that anticipated further development. *Courtesy of the National Park Service, Frederick Law Olmsted National Historic Site*

approximately the size of the original development in the British Properties. The layout is different, and the garden city is a much more complete community, but these basics are strikingly similar.

The Olmsted brothers, whose father Frederick Olmsted was the father of modern American landscape architecture, were hired to design the property, with James Dawson head landscape architect. Their property

was a blank canvas, mostly devoid of people or buildings, on which they could paint their masterpiece. The original drawings include shops on either side of Taylor Way just below the Mount Moyne entrance, scrapped, says former president Jim McLean, because they thought the topography in this area was too ruggedly difficult for building. Other plans called for a polo field, riding stable and track southeast of the present golf course.

These elaborate plans were modified (Spuraway's riding stables were not far away), but it was still designed for an elite market. A letter from BPP dated January 25, 1938, notes that "all plans for buildings to be erected must be passed by our architectural committee and conform

This elevation shows a detail of the quaint market shops planned for Mount Moyne Plaza. Had they been built, there might not have been a Park Royal as we know it today. *Courtesy of the National Park Service, Frederick Law Olmsted National Historic Site*

to the standard set by the company, which will be artistic rather than monetary." Names of all roads were selected in England. The original title of Capilano Estates for the development didn't catch on; British Pacific Properties is how it was known from the early days. Although BPP is owned through a holding company, about half of the board members are from the Guinness family, visiting Canada frequently for board meetings.

Leyland and the representatives of BPP were very much on the same page. In a letter to W. Elgie Bland dated March 14, 1932, Leyland writes of "re-planning West Vancouver to the natural contour of the land so that the older portion would be in line with the new development that will be carried out by the English syndicate." All very well, but changing the location of streets after they're in is another matter. BPP has pursued its development generally separately from that of the rest of West Vancouver, although they remain in close communication. The predominantly

Perhaps to impress their British clients, in 1934 the Olmsteds designed model homes for the development in the style of this Tudor revival mansion. But by the time any substantial home building took place after the Second World War, such "old world" aesthetic values were less prominent. Modernism became the preferred style of the new post-war affluent middle class. *Courtesy of the National Park Service, Frederick Law Olmsted National Historic Site*

pre–Second World War grid pattern remains in flatter Ambleside and Dundarave, although the streets in other areas are necessarily more contoured to the land.

Reeve Leyland drove a hard bargain with the Guinness representative: "If you are not prepared to spend more than a million dollars on the Club House and the Golf Course we are not interested in that phase of the matter." The company complied, and the Capilano Golf Club opened for play in the summer of 1938. From BPP's point of view, the golf course enabled the creation of a park-like effect for the development without sacrificing valuable land. It was meticulously designed by the legendary Stanley Thompson, whose firm had built over a hundred golf courses, including those in Banff and Jasper, as exclusive clubs for the benefit of

For the entrance to the British Properties, at the top to Taylor Way, the Olmsted brothers depicted, in 1932, an American designer's version of a majestic British plaza, complete with fountains, Baroque statuary and old-world architecture. Today, although it is officially still called Mount Moyne Square, it consists only of a featureless roundabout. *Courtesy of the National Park Service, Frederick Law Olmsted National Historic Site*

the alpha males who were expected to populate the British Properties. Entrance fees were $150 for men and $100 for women, with annual fees of $100 and $55, respectively. The clubhouse was made suitably palatial,

as it was designed to be the Guinnesses' refuge if war or other factors made living conditions in England untenable.

The Capilano Golf and Country Club was established on December 28, 1938, with BPP collecting all dues and paying all bills. On April 1, 1955, BPP sold these assets to a new company named the Capilano Golf and Country Club (1955) Ltd. At this time, the Guinness family's assets were divided, with the Moyne branch taking BPP. They remain guardians of their conservative upper-class image; on the upper floor of

A monumental grand edifice with broad staircases, terraces and fountains was envisioned for the north side of the plaza, called Mount Moyne Park, after Walter Edward Guinness, 1st Baron Moyne, one of the major investors in the development. Instead, visitors have had to settle for a bus stop and a somewhat outdated kiosk with a faded map of the roads. *Courtesy of the National Park Service, Frederick Law Olmsted National Historic Site*

the clubhouse, jeans, exercise wear and "any bottoms that sit above mid-thigh" are among wear deemed unacceptable. Early golfing videos show many of the players nattily attired in shirts and ties.

The new housing development generated intense local interest. "Velvety lawns of lovely landed estates smile at the sun . . . where flowers splash their varied colours among the gardens that border the walks. . . . Here, indeed, a place that might be called 'a Paradise for the Gods' on a mountainside, yet traversed by smooth wide roads." "This [community] was built for the future, with meticulous care and with not one single detail of future requirement overlooked. It stands in the midst of a forest in an area where the rumble of machinery in factories and their smoking stacks *are forever banned.*"[49] BPP purchased Japanese cherry trees from Seattle for fifty cents each to line the Taylor Way approach. Their glorious early blossoms are still a welcome harbinger of spring.

And what of the women? Not all would be keen golfers. So how to attract them? Of course, some of the owners may have thought, they

would all want to go shopping. Perhaps this was part of the impulse behind building the first stage of Park Royal in 1950 to encourage families to buy homes on the North Shore. Perhaps the alpha males would be easier to attract to the frontiers, but women who might otherwise be marooned in their sylvan retreats could best be lured by high-end shopping. In the days before two cars were a part of life for those in the affluent middle class, BPP subsidized small shuttles to ferry residents between their homes and the new shopping centre, while their husbands were out slaying dragons in the corporate world. The new shopping centre proved an effective way of promoting housing sales.

The low density of the properties themselves was generally insufficient to support commercial activity, limiting the type of interaction that may have pointed it toward being more of a community of neighbours. The low density and large lots led to sizable areas where neighbourhoods and communities did not develop. It's not possible to meet your neighbour at a corner store when there are no corner stores. This is an important feature of BPP's coming Cypress Village, for here much of the emphasis is on fostering community, and much of the recent development in West Vancouver, such as Hollyburn Mews, tries to recreate the ambience of earlier neighbourhoods. In a talk to council in 1977, former president Peter Finch noted that BPP was hampered by its exclusively residential nature. It should, he said, be more than a bedroom community for commuters. The "suggested pattern for city development is through much more self-contained satellite communities." He criticized many residents' selfish resistance to change. "Now that I am here let us stop anyone else from enjoying the benefits of a house in this community." The company offered to donate three acres for a clubhouse and tennis and badminton courts, but the residents were not receptive and this donation did not proceed.

A list of restrictions, dated July 30, 1937, ratified at a meeting between Capilano Estates Limited and the Vancouver Real Estate Exchange, confirmed it as a subdivision of single-family homes with no business or advertising signs allowed. No barriers such as sidewalks, fences and hedges were allowed, as they wished to recreate the feeling of a British common. Most famously, the race exclusions initially made this a whites-only enclave. "No person of the African or Asiatic race or of African or Asiatic descent (except servants of the occupier of the premises in residence) shall reside or be allowed to remain on the premises." Jews, while not mentioned, were also excluded. Other Vancouver communities had similar exclusion policies, as overt racism was deeply engrained in Canadian society at this time. In 1921 West Vancouver council had passed a resolution denying "Orientals" the right to own property in their community.

Race restrictions not only limited the purchase of property but barred the hiring of non-Caucasians on such projects as the building of the Lions Gate Bridge and working in the North Shore shipyards before the Second World War. Some recall petitions against allowing Chinese to live in BPP being circulated in the 1950s. These restrictions slowly faded, and, from the first, the exclusion in BPP was soft pedalled. An early brochure omits any mention of this covenant. It is not on the list of exclusions for Blocks 39 and 40, which are northwest of the original BPP development, north of Crestline Road. A 1961 issue of the newsletter, *The Tally Ho*, lists the covenants, although an asterisk by the side of the racial covenant indicates it has no legal effect.

With their limited access to the professions and to high-paying jobs generally, few homegrown Asians would have had the wealth needed to purchase in this area, even if they were allowed. Making the properties an area of upscale single-family homes was in itself enough to exclude minorities for many years. And then one might also ask how many would want to move in to a community where they might be viewed as unwelcome aliens?

The influx of Asians, which gathered impetus with the return of Hong Kong to China in 1997, and the migration of many Asian nationals to Canada in recent years have redrawn the local demographic map. Because much of the recent growth of West Vancouver has been in the British Properties, a higher percentage of newcomers reside there than in the rest of West Vancouver. In 1997, the Jewish presence asserted itself when the Har-El (Mountain of God) Synagogue opened on BPP land at 1305 Taylor Way. However, even as progress becomes encouragingly apparent, evidence of racism persists: while construction was underway, a spray-painted swastika disfigured a construction sign, along with the slogan "Juden Raus," which means "Jews Out," the name of a board game created as anti-Semitic propaganda in 1930s Germany.

A Bridge to Somewhere

> Light and graceful, like a spider's web in the sun.
>
> —Joe LePage, bridge worker

Communication links have always been crucial to the viability of West Vancouver. John Lawson and his three partners created their ferry company in 1909 to provide access to their property and enhance its value. *West Vancouver No. 1, Sea Foam* and other vessels provided pleasant ways of transporting people to and from Vancouver. Just as the ferries of the early years defined the bucolic early waterfront existence, Lions Gate Bridge later provided communication suitable to a community of the established affluent.

The Second Narrows Bridge (1925) theoretically provided a road link to Vancouver, but frequent collisions between the bridge and ships caught up in the powerful currents churning through the Second

Narrows led it to languish damaged and unused for long periods of time. A major collision put it out of commission from 1930 to 1934, which greatly concerned Reeve Leyland and many others in the West Vancouver community. The community needed a more dependable connection between the growing North Shore and the Lower Mainland to protect its investments.

The north end of the Lions Gate Bridge landed squarely in the centre of Capilano Reserve, but, as elsewhere, the wishes of the Indigenous in regard to their land were ignored. Negotiations for this land took place between the First Narrows Bridge Company and the Committee of the Privy Council. No direct consultation with the Squamish took place.[50]

The British Properties brought the necessary financial backing for the new bridge over the First Narrows, which would enhance the accessibility and value of their land, as it was expected (rightly) that most BPP males would work in Vancouver. Entrepreneur A.J. Taylor was an ardent supporter of and fundraiser for the bridge. In December 1931 he arranged for the Guinness-led syndicate to acquire a controlling interest in the First Narrows Bridge Company, which merged two firms that had been granted bridge charters in June 1930; both he and the West Vancouver municipality wanted a four-lane bridge, but more conservative views prevailed. Taylor had a penchant for going big, and about 1939 conceived plans for a revolving restaurant on Sentinel Hill, designed by architect Theo Korner (which was not built).

Considering it was a gift, the bridge had a surprisingly difficult time getting approved. The CPR opposed it, as BPP's plans rivalled its own for upscale housing developments in Shaughnessy, not to mention that Canadian Prime Minister R.B. Bennett was a director of the CPR. West Vancouver municipal solicitor Gordon Robson stated that the CPR called the captains of the Empress liners to declare that it was unsafe to have a bridge across the First Narrows because it might, in time of war, block the entrance to Vancouver Harbour. Vancouver City Council, conscious of the CPR's clout, also turned down the bridge, and it looked as if the project, and the housing development that depended on it, would fall apart before it got started.

Reeve Leyland, impatient with the "typically English cricket campaign" the BPP was waging to promote their project, lined up thirty-five prominent Vancouver citizens to appear before council in support of the bridge. Vancouver council agreed to hold a referendum. Leyland took out full-page ads in the newspapers and rented two vacant businesses in Vancouver as campaign headquarters, buying up nearly all the available time on four city radio stations to promote the building of the bridge. Future Vancouver mayor Gerry McGeer gave a spellbinding speech during the last hour of the broadcasting schedule the night before voting day. The referendum passed comfortably, 17,806 to 7,615, on December 13, 1933.

But the Canadian government still had to be convinced. Leyland visited Ottawa, where he spent a week pursuing Prime Minister Bennett and navigating the bureaucracy he found so frustrating. Although he received no commitment for support at this time, the Canadian government finally gave its assent April 29, 1936, with an order-in-council stipulating no Chinese labourers could be used in construction. This may have been moved along by Bennett's defeat by Mackenzie King in the October 1935 election. BPP's Lord Southborough obtained low rates for bridge financing, contingent on the use of British steel.[51]

Leyland delayed the final signing of the agreement until the bridge solicitors inserted a clause allowing West Vancouver to run its own bus transportation system over the span into Vancouver, and in 1940 Leyland's successor, Reeve J. Edward Sears, and council passed a bylaw to purchase four new buses. That's why the blue buses run over Lions Gate Bridge to Vancouver today. The bus service has continued to be a proud feature of West Vancouver life; in 1996 West Vancouver transit became the first in Canada to have a fleet of wheelchair-accessible buses.

On November 12, 1938, a victorious Leyland stood in the centre of the bridge and shook hands with Vancouver mayor George C. Miller to mark its opening to pedestrian traffic; it opened to cars two days later. This was, coincidentally, almost exactly a year after the other major Lower Mainland bridge of the time, the Pattullo Bridge (soon to be replaced), had opened on November 15, 1937. Just as the latter connected New Westminster with Surrey to the south, the Lions Gate Bridge affirmed Vancouver's northern connections. Leyland was sure that "with the construction of the First Narrows Bridge . . . the North Shore will become a revitalised district" very much in the British tradition. At the official opening of the Lions Gate Bridge by King George VI on May 26, 1939, Leyland announced, "West Vancouver is a community, essentially British in its outlook, composed of people who respect law and order, who love that peace and freedom which only democracies enjoy and who

On November 12, 1938, Reeve Leyland, along with Vancouver mayor George Miller, a radio reporter and a group of excited youngsters gaze upward in awe. The object of their wonderment is not the bridge itself, but a photographer dangling off a girder to get a picture of the historic proceedings. *West Vancouver Museum and Archives, 123.WVA.LEY*

are proud of the traditions of the race from which they spring."[52] Tolls for each car were a reasonable twenty-five cents.

At the bridge's southern entrance, regal British lions, cast by Canadian sculptor Charles Marega, express a stately power and control. They are echoed by the more passionate Chinese imperial lions that grace the entrance to Vancouver's Chinatown on Pender Street, and to a number of other Vancouver buildings. In a curious connection with the Lions Gate lions, A.J. Taylor placed his baby shoes in one of them. He also wanted both lions' tails to be visible to anyone crossing the bridge; he had two moulds for the tails made, so one lion's tail would be on the left side and the other on the right.

The bridge also drove development of North Vancouver. During the Second World War, thousands of shipyard workers used the bridge daily to reach their work at Burrard Dry Dock and North Van Ship Repair. Housing development after the war also boomed. Capilano Highlands

With increased development came increased traffic to West Van. Resulting congestion called for the construction, in the 1950s, of a clover-leaf approach to replace the simple intersection at the north end. Cartoonist Al Beaton made fun of the local angst about invasive freeways. *Estate of Allan Beaton*

developed in the northwest of the District of North Vancouver, in many ways similar to the British Properties in much of its architecture, although aimed at a less affluent clientele. By 1950, 1,200 lots selling for an affordable \$575 to \$775 were developed. Modernist architect Fred Hollingsworth designed about fifty homes here. Down the hill, just east of the Capilano Reserve, Norgate developed 480 homes between 1949 and 1952 on land that had previously been designated for a private airport. Carpenter William Thomas Hullah's construction company mass-produced fifty houses at a time in a Ford assembly-line manner. Small but attractive ranch-style homes, they incorporated many new technologies to fulfill the affordable dreams of an emerging post-war middle class.

The opening of the bridge precipitated the decline of the ferries from West Vancouver to Vancouver, which ended service February 8, 1947. From the beginning, the bridge was heavily used: 3,390 cars a day in 1939 increased to 20,224 per day by 1953. In 1951, the *Province* reported that a special constable had been hired to handle the traffic problems. "[We are] approaching the day when it [the bridge] will no longer be adequate to handle the great flood of traffic."[53] A New York consulting engineer recommended building a second span next to the first. Instead, in 1952 BPP and the municipality chose the cheaper option of converting the two-lane bridge to three perilously narrow lanes, designed by West Vancouver engineer Ed Richardson.

The provincial government saw ownership of the bridge as essential to ensuring public service. When BC premier W.A.C. Bennett's initial offer to purchase it was refused, he said, very well, he would build another bridge. But that didn't happen. Instead, the BC government bought the bridge in 1955, abolished all tolls on April 1, 1963, and implemented lane-control signals in 1964, with the centre lane alternating directions according to the traffic.

Spurred by ever-increasing traffic, plans for a third crossing, whether a bridge or tunnel, have been the subject of endless debate. In 1954 the bridge company acquired rights to nine acres of Squamish land to the east of the present bridge in anticipation of another crossing. Proposals for a third crossing initially emerged in the late 1960s, but met with strenuous resistance from some West Vancouverites who feared it would lead to a major increase in their population. A 1969 report recommended a twin bridge with a tunnel through Stanley Park connecting to both bridges; it was narrowly defeated, perhaps partly because the plans for linking freeway construction in Vancouver had been rejected. A 1970 report by Swan Wooster, commissioned by West Vancouver, also recommended a third crossing, but in 1972 the less development-oriented NDP ousted the Social Credit government and shelved all proposals.

In the mid-1990s, political and public interests again raised the question of a new link. Over fifteen designs were on the table, including a tunnel, multiple decks, multiple lanes and a twinned bridge. None were considered viable. Some creative ideas included double-decking the bridge, with three lanes going each way; and dredging a tunnel and dumping the fill off Stanley Park, which would create an island that could then be sold to developers. Architect Arthur Erickson argued for the tunnel, but at a cost of $600 million and rising, he failed to acquire sufficient support. Plans for a third crossing ran up against some intransigent problems, chiefly the managing of several lanes of traffic disgorging onto city streets at either end of a bridge or tunnel.

Instead, renovation of the current structure was seen as the only viable option, with plans to replace the deck and modify the bridge's overall structure beginning in 1998. The contract was jointly awarded to American Bridge and West Vancouver–based Surespan, with the two-year construction costing $124.9 million. The main bridge deck was replaced in 2000–01, the first time this had been done on a suspension bridge. Fifty-four deck sections, each weighing about a hundred tonnes and ten and twenty metres in length, with structural framing under them, had to be hoisted out using special hydraulic equipment. Fifteen complicated steps were required for each section, which caused many traffic disruptions but no serious incidents. The changes allowed the dangerously narrow, unprotected pedestrian/bicycle sidewalks to be moved to the outside of the structure and widened from 1.2 metres to 2.7 metres, with traffic lanes widened from 3 metres to 3.6 metres. The renovated bridge is expected to be good for another eighty years.

In 2013, the nineteen-deck *Celebrity Solstice,* one of the world's newest and tallest cruise ships, had its mast altered so it could be retracted to fit under the Lions Gate Bridge. Although raising the bridge was feasible, modifying the masts or funnels of cruise ships was cheaper.

For now, all other plans remain in abeyance. The traffic has been somewhat ameliorated by the Seabus, which began service in June of 1977, and may be alleviated in the future by rapid transit. Still, between 60,000 and 70,000 vehicles now cross on an average workday, as the rush hour continues to expand, often causing interminable delays. But it is now accepted wisdom that more road access increases the number of cars, so building another bridge would not solve the traffic problem.

In its early days, some naysayers derided the Lions Gate as a bridge to nowhere—hardly a consideration now. But for the most part, it's hard to overestimate the civic pride the bridge evoked at the time it was built, especially in the days following its completion. A souvenir book evoked the romantic pleasures of the spectacular view:

> *At night the scene is one of breath-taking beauty in its sheer loveliness, the lights of the ship reflected in the water, passing on their lawful occasions, almost, it would seem, at your feet, with the glittering panorama of the lights of the city mirrored in the water gives one the feeling that this sight alone, more than repays one for the journey.*

The First Steps

> I know of no place where one may so combine proximity to a large and interesting city with all the advantages of country life.
> —Poet A.M. Stephens (1929)

By 1937 construction of infrastructure and the golf course had cost the British Properties $1.5 million, well above the $1 million they had contracted for with the purchase of the land. But slow sales concerned the investors. The original design called for 450 lots of a sizable 1.29 acres each, priced from $5,600 to $20,000. This was at the high end of the Vancouver market, and few lots sold before the Second World War. Sales were hardly helped by only a third of the lots being serviced by both water and power as of 1939. Even the new bridge didn't help: by 1946, only seventy houses had been built.

After the war, BPP rethought the development. Initially the road system wound through a dense forest of trees, which made views problematic. P.D. (Perry) Willoughby, BPP's managing director for twenty-four years, has been credited by many for a vision that led to the project's success. Under his direction, in 1945 the BPP engaged Alexander Walker (Vancouver) and Hugh Russell (Seattle), who had wide experience in planning and subdivision, to make recommendations concerning planning development. They suggested:

- Smaller lots
- Widespread clearing of trees to improve views
- Acquisition of property for a shopping centre

The BPP followed all recommendations. In place of 450 lots, they created 1,300, selling for $900 to $7,500. This greatly added to the development costs, as many roads required rebuilding and some water mains had to be changed, but it was worth it. Sales greatly increased, with modest cedar bungalows selling for an affordable $15,000 to $20,000. Willoughby's obituary credits him with "The transformation of the Properties from a paradise for non-existent millionaires to a fine residential district for people in a wide range of income brackets."[54] Notwithstanding, he thought the land could have been better used.

Etta and Joseph Leyland don their finest for their brush with royalty in 1939. King George VI and Queen Elizabeth would visit West Vancouver to take a cup of tea at the top of the British Properties, attracting attention to, and no doubt conferring regal status upon, the new development. *West Vancouver Museum and Archives, 188.WVA.LEY, Barclays Photographers*

Onslow Place, Midhurst Place and parts of other streets had frontage on only one side.

The British Properties has often developed show homes for promotional purposes. The first of these was the company cottage designed by William Bow, where the British king and queen savoured cups of tea and the gorgeous view, built in 1935 as a show home and sales centre. A few years later, the 1948 Kenwood "House of Ideas," the first home on Fairmile Drive, with five functional rooms, showed what could be had for $11,500. Completely decorated and furnished by Spencer's Interior Decorators in a Chinese-modern decorating scheme, a brochure described its "free and easy spaciousness created with the incorporation of outside grounds and interior by the extensive use of glass, the patio, [and] the sun deck [which] seems to double the living area." Six electric kitchen appliances included a garbage disposal and a dishwasher. State-of-the-art amenities included a built-in bar, a built-in shower with ultra-violet lamps and wall-to-wall carpeting. Gardens and a southern exposure enhanced its attractiveness. The house remained open for two summers, drawing visitors in record numbers and successfully promoting BPP as the place to live.

Royalty arrives for tea. In what must have been a first in celebrity endorsements, Her Majesty, Queen Elizabeth, preceded by George VI and escorted by Mounties, makes her way up to the highest home in the British Properties for a cup of tea and a view over the commoners below. A royal visit to a new housing development would have conferred a status that must have been the envy of developers everywhere.
City of Vancouver Archives, CVA 6–92

The elegant Muriel May, often referred to at the time as "the world's most glamorous real estate woman," was BPP's hugely successful salesperson from 1947 to 1960, no doubt helped by the building of the Park Royal Shopping Centre and Canada's surging economy. A trailblazer in many ways, May was a single mother who had borrowed $100 in 1942 to take a business course at Sprott Shaw Business College. In November 1944, Arnold Shook of Shook Realty asked her to work for him, and in 1947 Willoughby asked her to take over as sales representative for the properties. Over the next two years she travelled widely throughout North America promoting their development, her pleasant appearance front and centre in many ads. In 1949 a New York industrialist flew in to buy six lots for a total of $19,600, which went a long way to giving the company credibility. A multi-page spread on the British Properties in the October 1950 issue of the new magazine *Western Homes and Living* certainly did no harm. "What a place to bring the little woman" commented one local. And how would Ms. May have responded to that?

Times have changed, and methods and standards of construction

By 1954, houses being built in the properties were modern in style, designed to take in the panoramic views over the city. *West Vancouver Memorial Library, WVML.3352.PR, Don Coltman photo*

have come a long way. In the original development, the streets were edgeless paved lanes with wiring strung on poles and water mains made of four-inch (ten-centimetre) wood stave pipes—far too small. Bringing all this up to current standards took many years, with BPP evolving with our social expectations and technical knowledge as the frontier of construction brought new homes to the rugged terrain.

Moving West

For most of the last century, development of land in the northern parts of West Vancouver was slow. Reeve Morgan had made some initial moves in this direction in 1921, but it was left to BPP to undertake the first major development. The Upper Levels highway, first officially suggested in the 1945 Harland Bartholomew report, was completed in 1957 and expanded to a four-lane divided highway between 1971 and 1974, with land expropriated from the properties for the parts of the highway that passed through BPP. It skirted the southern edge of the properties, serving both as access to the western areas of West Vancouver and a route to points north.

> To one gent, regret that we don't know of any rich widows with nasty coughs.[55]

The municipality suggested that accompanying infrastructure should include the creation of self-contained residential areas north of the highway, including parks, schools and commercial areas. Required student space was projected at twenty-seven classrooms for elementary students and eleven for high school; commercial sites (gas stations, hotels) along the highway were also planned. Most of this didn't happen, with the British Properties retaining its residential purity, the highway remaining a barrier that reinforced the seclusion and even isolation of their land. A 1956 municipal study looked forward to the shape of the new community north of the highway, calling for the continuation of single-family homes, which would have only one kitchen and no more than two lodgers.

Development of Chartwell began in 1962 and continued over the next twenty years, followed by Canterbury in 1992. The latter, overseen by Walter Thorneloe, was developed on the western edge of the initial developed area. Here houses larger than those in the original development made their appearance. Further west, Westhill, at the top of 21st Street, the smaller developments of Almondel and Rockridge, below the Upper Levels Highway, and Cypress Ridge, just above it, were also completed between 1959 and 1990. Gradually other housing forms found their way beyond the drawing board. While in 1974 BPP manager Peter Finch planned to develop the land between the Chartwell and Cammeray subdivisions and Lawson Creek in accordance with existing single-family guidelines, land between Lawson and McDonald Creeks was earmarked for possible cluster housing. These were groupings of homes, typically sharing walls and exterior maintenance and landscaping, which thus allowed more land for open space. The Citizens' Planning Forum favoured cluster housing as the best way to create a sense of community, preserve green space, avoid flood hazards and implement sound planning techniques.[56]

Early residents had restrictive ideas of development, often opposing trails through their area even though they would be built on municipal land. In 1983 TV host David Mulligan noted, "I have never seen anyone walking in the British Properties." That may have been partly because early developments did not permit sidewalks. Changes were difficult. Willoughby noted that in the original BPP agreements, "Once a subdivision plan had been registered and subject to a restrictive covenant, the consent of every lot owner to a commercial zoning became necessary, and the defect was almost impossible to remedy."

> There is no truth to the rumour that BPP is including a lifetime supply of Guinness Stout with all lot sales.[57]

Many moving to the properties have brought with them quite an astonishing sense of entitlement. In 1975 local homeowner Alan Jessup unsuccessfully argued that BPP residents should get special garbage collection because they "pay higher taxes but get the same level of municipal services such as fire and police protection." He and some other residents wanted to leave their garbage at the top of their driveways rather than take it to the curbside like the West Vancouver residents in other areas who paid less in taxes. But the infrastructure for the large homes and rugged topography of the properties was far more expensive than for the flatter areas of Ambleside and Dundarave.

On April 8, 1974, Peter Finch wrote a memo to council suggesting that the planning process include all stakeholders. This more collaborative approach did not take firm root until the development of Whitby Estates around the turn of this century, when Jim McLean became president, but has continued since, with extensive community meetings and other opportunities for residents and others to provide input.

Although most West Vancouverites during the late 1970s wanted little or no growth, some had other visions. In July 1973 council released a report suggesting that the British Properties employ a combination of housing that would highlight cluster-type development, and set a maximum overall density of three units per acre. This indicated the possibility that 13,000 to 18,000 residents might be added to the properties alone, and many local ratepayers feared the extensive changes this would mean for their community. In reality, the overall population of West Vancouver as a whole has increased by fewer than 7,000 since then, so most of the feared changes never saw daylight. Although this project did not materialize, in the ensuing years plans for modest higher density made their way beyond the drawing board. The single-family home was no longer the only answer.

In about 1990 plans were floated for a twenty-seven-lot subdivision at the end of Tyrol Place in Chartwell. Nearby resident Khosrow Kaye was one of those objecting at a public hearing. "We did not move to this area to get affordable housing." The average size of these planned homes was 2,300 square feet, considerably larger than many of the earlier modernist homes.

Others dreamed of a Hollywood North in West Vancouver. Beginning in 1957 Oldrich Vaclavek planned to populate the forty-seven-acre site above the present Salmon House with film studios and an elaborate supportive infrastructure, known as Panorama Film Studios. Plans called for television studios, processing laboratories and a recording studio. A luxury lodge, club, residences and a nine-hole golf course were also planned. As Canadian TV stations were now required to schedule more programming with Canadian content, the timing was thought to be auspicious. BPP salesperson Muriel May became involved as a principal shareholder.

The studios had some modest successes, particularly with the TV show "Let's Make a Deal," but bringing in Tom Jones to produce a lavish musical spectacular proved disastrous. Major cost overruns led to bankruptcy in 1981, although by this time the area's transformation into Panorama Estates was complete.

West Vancouver locations have often been used for films. Pat Burns had dreams of a film studio on Harvey Haddon's property, and a half century later *McCabe & Mrs. Miller* was filmed in Cypress Park Estates and Cypress Falls Park. The Arthur Erickson–designed home at 118 Stevens Drive was the setting for the vampire family Cullens in *Twilight* and *New Moon*. More recently, fans of the popular TV series *Real Housewives of Vancouver* may recognize scenes from Whitby Estates' Twin Creek Place.

In 1959, Gil Bradner and Fred Russell formed the International Land Corporation (ILC), which developed a number of West Vancouver properties including Spuraway, the Seastrand, Wedgewood Terrace and Bayridge. With the support of Lord Folkestone, the company purchased twenty-six acres that became the residential development Panorama Estates on part of the property that had been Panorama Film Studios. Lengthy negotiations and revisionings with the municipality began in 1968 and extended over several years. Many feared that this development would spur multi-unit construction above the Upper Levels Highway. When council argued for funding to defray the costs of services such as sewers, water and flood control necessitated by the increased density, ILC donated $300,000 to the municipality.[58] Begun in 1973 and completed in 1980, Panorama's tiered levels remain one of the most visible developments to anyone driving north across the Lions Gate Bridge.

Commercial development played a substantial part in early plans, in one proposal consisting of four stores, a gas station and a restaurant, but mostly it didn't happen. In an agreement between the district and Toseki Entertainment Ltd., Units 101 and 102 of the Salmon House were designated as space for a convenience store. This has not happened; some thought a convenience store would bring "undesirables" to the community, or perhaps the perceived business was insufficient. In any case, a corner store above the highway has never existed, although several other sites have been zoned for convenience stores that have never happened.

Precipitated by the Panorama proposal, staff and council formed a committee in 1973 to bring in a clear development policy for the

Upper Lands. Through its land-use contracts, West Vancouver was able to require dedication of land for purposes such as parks, schools and open space. Development policies, refined following the 1976 Sutton-Brown report, required that development be kept below the 1,200-foot (364-metre) level, and that the integrity of creeks be respected. Storm water runoff was to be minimized, and natural drainage courses were not to be diverted. Protecting the natural integrity of the environment through provision of greenbelts was key. Peter Jones, mayor from 1974 to 1978, was a main driver of these developments.

Gradually, apartments outside the Ambleside area broke the pattern of single-family homes in the Upper Lands. At Deer Ridge, the first apartment buildings (ten storeys), along with seventy-five townhomes, were built above the highway in 1996. Sixty per cent of the property remains virtually undeveloped, with natural drainage patterns preserved. As landscape architect Harry Haggard commented, "The final plan was to be in harmony with nature as much as possible." In 2002, BPP approved Stonecliff, to be developed by Concert Properties on land just west of Deer Ridge into three fifteen-storey apartment buildings on Cypress Bowl Road, with thirty-seven units in each building.

Whitby Estates

When Jim McLean became president of BPP in 1999, he found the company a quiet operation, staffed by a small group of dedicated employees but selling only a few lots a year. He changed all that, introducing a more proactive management style and coordinated development. McLean ensured that every lot sold would increase the value of the next lot. Covenants enhanced the development of each area, while design guidelines controlled the appearance of the houses. This brought a consistency to the appearance, but not much room for quirky individualism, as former director of planning Steve Nicholls noted. The trade-off between community values and the expression of individual personality continues.

Council approved Whitby Estates, north of Panorama Village between McDonald and Marr Creeks, in July 1999. As of 2017, 130 single-family homes and 66 townhomes had been completed. Original plans that called for clear-cutting were modified; tree removal was to be allowed only near a lot's driveway access. An important stipulation was that builders were required to build within two years of purchasing their land, preventing lots from sitting unused.

From the 1940s until 1999, BPP had not been involved directly in building houses, preferring to sell the land to owners or to speculative builders who worked out building plans with the future owners. As Lythe Court in Whitby Estates neared completion, the properties ventured back into construction, building 10 to 20 per cent of the houses in this development. In subsequent developments BPP has taken a hands-on approach, assuming complete control of building and development through their division, British Pacific Homes.

Some people were not the best stewards of their property, as the seclusion made some houses great locations for grow ops. In the first three months of 2000, ten homes in BPP were raided for pot growing. Some had been rented and were poorly maintained, with overgrown lawns and piles of debris being subjects of complaints from their neighbours. Fortunately for the appearance and respectability of BPP, growing grass has decreased, and cutting it has increased in recent years.

Development plans by BPP are now accompanied by numerous public forums and published presentations, gauging and informing public opinion long before the backhoes start moving dirt. Ecological concerns have assumed prime importance. Thirteen major creeks, and the unique ecological and historical features of the area, have received detailed research. Greenbelts and parks have been developed, as well as walkways and bike routes. By the time the Rodgers Creek subdivision went up, interconnecting trails were an uncontroversial and integral part of the plan, and even sidewalks made an appearance, although often on only one side of the street.

Children, along with researchers, initiated a successful protest to protect McDonald Creek's coastal tailed frog, the only frog found in fast-flowing streams. From 1998 to 2003, researchers studied the frogs intensively, recommending such measures for their preservation as anti-pollution devices installed in the storm sewers and larger streamside setbacks. Research has found that when development proceeds in this way, the frog population does not diminish in this stream or others in the area. Researchers are also monitoring fish, wildlife, birds and other amphibians. Setbacks to streams are varied in accordance with its natural inhabitants and the nature of the ravine.

Rodgers Creek

James Rodgers's Tower Hill farm, located near the top of 29th Street, gave its name to Rodgers Creek, and this extensive development in turn became its namesake. It consists of 215 acres from Marr Creek to Cave Creek between the Cypress Bowl Highway and the 1,200-foot (364-metre) level. The properties own all but twenty acres, which four other individuals own in five-acre parcels. The properties incorporated more green space and less clear-cutting in this development, with smaller houses and more varied residential development.

Planning for this area, which got underway in 2000, includes the elucidation of principles that will guide the development of the adjacent Cypress Village; the two areas will be developed as an integrated community. In November and December 2005, BPP initiated two one-day "envisioning workshops," which identified three key directions that would distinguish the future Upper Lands neighbourhoods. These were: A vibrant village centre; a mountain path connecting the village and other Upper Lands neighbourhoods; and a diversified housing model to reflect the principles of sustainable development.

This project proceeded with great enthusiasm from the participants. Mark Holland of the Holland Barrs Planning Group saw it as "a leading example of increased density and housing diversity on land that absorbs growth pressures while preserving trees, creeks and the region's farm land."[59]

The "envisioning notebook," called "Building a Sustainable Strategy for the Future," laid out eight pillars for the development and presented them to West Vancouver Council and staff in May 2006. This report emphasizes the critical concern with the environment. Geoff Croll, the current manager, considered that BPP was always ahead of its time in this regard. "If you compare the pattern of development within the original British Properties with areas that were developed at the same time below the highway by others, you will notice that below the highway there is much more encroachment into the riparian areas of creeks to the point where many creeks are literally in flumes running between homes and watercourses are more likely to be in pipes." This concern has become better integrated with current development plans.

In January 2007 council appointed a group of nine independent citizens as the Rodgers Creek Area Plan Working Group to oversee the plan. Over the next fourteen months, planners, architects, engineers and others established the key organizing principles, provided direction on key issues and reviewed evolving versions of the area plan. They held two public open houses with a number of meetings that included recreational users and district staff. A consensus emerged that "the land informs the site." Developer, council and community worked together to, as mayor Pam Goldsmith-Jones said, build "a more sustainable community in West Vancouver."

Environmental studies by Sartori Environmental Services proposed new standards. Environmental enhancement included the establishment of a number of new wetlands, which provide low-maintenance habitat for amphibians, birds and insects. "In the event that an active songbird nest is discovered, a 20m radius buffer will be flagged in field, and no cleaning works or machinery operations will be conducted within the radius until SES confirms that the nest is no longer active."[60]

A vision for a sustainable mountainside community, planned and presented to district council in April 2008, included detailed technical analysis of slopes, an inventory of vegetation and ecosystems, an assessment of all water courses, and a detailed mapping of trails, recreation and cultural features. Developers clustered construction into six distinct areas within four neighbourhoods, with a wide range of recreation, community and residential amenities. "The new residential enclaves will be clustered within natural habitat corridors and linked together by green space in the form of parkland, trails and landscaped roads." Generous streamside setbacks for Marr and Rodgers Creeks protect wildlife. Over 55 per cent is protected green space, including "creeks and their riparian corridors, forest, rock bluffs." Buildings were to be placed on sites suitable for development, while areas unsuitable for building would remain green. Of the total of 736 units, only 14 per cent would be single-family homes. Another 70 per cent would be apartments and the remaining 16 per cent duplexes and townhouses. Green buildings, green infrastructure and planning for alternative modes of transportation would reduce environmental impact, with development designed to fit the land rather than the reverse.[61]

Geoff Croll expresses pride that the BPP builds the most energy-efficient homes in West Vancouver. The single-family homes consume

50 per cent less energy and emit 85 per cent less greenhouse gas than a similar home built to the BC building code, and 94 per cent less than the typical unrenovated 1960 West Vancouver home.

Croll is a local boy who grew up in Bayridge, graduating from UBC in civil engineering. He spent much of his youth enjoying the hills and trails of the North Shore; snowshoeing at night remains one of his delights. "If you go out at night, it's magical, with the light from the headlamps darting through the trees and reflecting off the snow." He brings a passionately held belief in both development and the environment to his work: "You can have development and preservation of these ecological, recreational values." A member of West Vancouver Streamkeepers, he participates actively in many of its projects. Before soliciting public opinion, BPP meets with streamkeepers and other stakeholders as appropriate, along with management, environmental consultants and engineers to analyze the site. BPP is also active in numerous other environmental initiatives.

Many innovations make the area more livable. Homes are designed with flat driveways, decreasing road parking. One bridge was made one lane, partly to lessen disturbance to the creek, but also, Croll says, to make the space more human—people would have to stop and interact with each other. Blasted rock and other materials are reused locally. Solar energy is expected to supply a sizable proportion of energy needs.

In January 2007, the municipality appointed a team of ten West Vancouver citizens with distinguished records in planning and development to guide the planning process, making the Rodgers Creek development community based rather than solely a BPP creation. Jim McLean and Walt Thorneloe represented BPP on the working group, which laid out guidelines for the future development of the western portion of the Upper Levels. Council approved the Rodgers Creek Area Development Plan in September 2008.

How much and what kind of density? The benchmark in BPP, as defined by the municipality, is 2.5 units per acre. The planned density of the new neighbourhoods varies to accommodate different types of housing according to the terrain, while retaining an overall density within municipal guidelines. In the eastern parts, the Chairlift and Mulgrave neighbourhoods have relatively low densities of under two units per acre, with the unused densities transferred to areas farther west. The Upper and Lower East Village neighbourhoods, located near the first switchback of the Cypress Bowl Road, sit on steeper slopes where single-family residences are not as viable. Plans here include higher-density areas: 10.5 units per acre for the Lower East Village and 4.83 for the Upper East Village. This density takes the whole area into account, including green space. Croll believes the density in the developed areas will be sufficient to attract public transit—essential, he says, to the viability of the project.

He sums up the planning process for this development as follows:

> *For the Rodgers Creek planning process, we established the total number of units allowed under the OCP (Official Community Plan) for the acreage which worked out to be 215 acres x 2.5 units per acre = 538 units. We established the building massing and floor area that would be generated by 538 units (1,875,670 square feet) and the Rodgers Creek Working Group then asked us to increase the number of units but keep the building massing and floor area the same which led to a plan with 736 units. In other words, we took the same building massing and floor area density and chopped it up into smaller units, which would provide a greater diversity of housing for the community. We then concentrated those 736 units in discrete development nodes which allowed us to conserve over 55% of the land area as protected green space.*

With his concept of "sieve analysis," Ian McHarg, author of *Design with Nature* (1969), developed a system of priorities to determine what can be developed with the least amount of impact on an area. His ideas have been influential in current environmental planning. BuiltGreen energy performance and sustainable construction techniques will drive the construction of new homes. Climate change is a wild card that will, one hopes, be adequately accommodated by drainage pipes that can deal with storm water in a once-in-two-hundred-years storm event.

Cypress Village: The Eve of Construction

Original plans for Cypress Village were generated under President Jim McLean when he took up his position in 1999. He looked at the inventory of land and saw that what was missing was a village centre. "The Village is envisioned as the heart and soul of the Cypress/Rodgers community. It is the essential component of realizing the goals of building sustainable communities on those Upper Lands . . . a destination for all of West Vancouver and will be recognized as the gateway to world class recreation."[62] Environmental best practices are again central, with narrower roads, fish ladders and LED street lighting planned. Creeks damaged by bad logging practices are being restored wherever possible.

The lands that will become Cypress Village are huge: 6,000 acres of undeveloped publicly and privately owned land above the highway, including the historic Hollyburn cabin area. About 4,600 acres sit above the 1,200-foot (364-metre) level (currently the upper limit acceptable for residential development), which is owned mostly by the district, and 1,400 acres lie below the 1,200-foot level, owned mostly by BPP. The proposed planning area for Cypress Village comprises 350 acres of mostly BPP land below the 1,200-foot level and 440 acres of BPP and district land above that level. Although the specifics are very much up for discussion, all possibilities include clustered development at the base of Cypress, with shops and services forming an appropriately scaled neighbourhood centre. One proposal includes an upper campus located above the 1,200-foot level, which would house educational, hospitality and employment opportunities, connected to the village by a gondola to minimize the use of cars.

In the interests of developing a community that is not just narrowly residential, and given that industry no longer necessarily means factories belching clouds of black smoke, it might be time to revisit West Vancouver's ban on industry. A Silicon Valley of the north has been suggested, as have film studios.

Although officially not allowed in most of West Vancouver, industry survives in some unusual shapes. Ray Wood lives with his wife Robyn Wenner in the basement of the Black Cat grocery, spending much of his time in his Land Rover travelling across Africa (three times) and Australia (twice). He has transformed many of these recent experiences into a novel, *Stalking Geraldine*. But even more remarkably, he manufactures overdrives for Land Rovers, making about a hundred a year from parts imported from the US, and machined by a lathe in his shop in the Black Cat. Designed as an extra gear, these give the vehicles better performance and economy.

Cypress Village will provide a unique gateway to mountain recreation, including a range of housing types and unit sizes for diverse ages, if not incomes. Schools, libraries, recreational centres and other facilities may appear, but chain stores or restaurants will not. Emphasis will be on retail outlets, such as bike shops and outdoor clothing shops, that relate to the outdoor experience. A 2016 working document explains that a "more concentrated mixed-use development helps to preserve more of the natural environment; it provides services for existing and future Upper Lands development that is accessible by foot, bike and transit; houses services that support and enhance the recreational activities in the Upper Lands; and offers a greater diversity of housing types and tenures."

Much of the undeveloped area is prime recreational land, with some of the best mountain-biking terrain anywhere. Liability and environmental damage from this sport have been concerns, and some hikers were also unhappy that bikers had usurped some of their hiking trails. In 1999, a young rider fell and was badly injured, leading to confrontation. The development of a Mountain Bike Task Force has mitigated this, leading to a more cooperative atmosphere, although the question of liability remains unresolved. The sport has gained respectability; many elite competitors who have honed their skills on the North Shore trails have gone on to achieve international success. Mountain biking forms an integral part of the vision for Cypress Village.

Adding up to 7,200 residents to West Vancouver's population over the next fifty years will create as many as 1,700 permanent jobs. More than a residential enclave from which people would commute to work, shopping or other services, Cypress Village could be an independent community and destination. Many people employed here could be driving or taking transit from elsewhere. As the 2008 Rodgers Creek Overview Report says, "Direct and easy access to the Village that does not depend on the automobile is key to achieving the objectives of the Official Community Plan for a more sustainable and complete community."[63] This could change the nature of living in the British Properties.

Numerous public discussions and a succession of publications have communicated the gradually emerging themes of the new development. The September 15, 2016, community discussion document suggests possibilities of "great trails, parks and natural spaces; educational facilities; community centre; shops; work spaces; a range of housing choices; health and wellness facilities; and hospitality uses all in a compact, walkable, transit-supportive environment."

The BPP has developed three potential scenarios for discussion purposes, all with a mix of single-family homes, condos, apartments and social outlets, and all including commercial spaces and some level of transit service. These are described in the community discussion document, although the numbers are far from fixed and vary slightly, even in the same document. The number of single-family homes is similar in all three plans, but the number of apartments varies greatly.

The smallest scenario is along the lines of North Vancouver's Edgemont Village, but remains a major development envisioning 1,800 units for 3,851 residents and providing 550 jobs. Most of the proposed development features apartments in buildings of up to sixteen storeys; however, 120 units would be single-family residences. This scenario also includes a variety of retail stores, a specialty grocer, a health clinic, restaurants/cafés and a ninety-room hotel.

The middle option would comprise 2,900 units for 5,662 residents, and provide 815 permanent jobs. Fewer than 120 units would be for single families, with the balance housing townhomes and apartments. In addition to the amenities in the first option, this option features a larger number of retail stores, restaurants/cafés, professional services and possibly an elementary school.

The Cadillac option, more on the scale of Port Moody's Newport Village or Vancouver's Olympic Village, plans for 3,800 units and 7,268 residents, providing 1,700 permanent jobs. Only 91 units would be single family, and the rest townhomes and apartments. Besides the amenities of the middle option, the larger population could facilitate more frequent transit service, destination dining, a small supermarket and a major employer, perhaps recreation, technology or sports related.

Working within their zoning parameters, the District of West Vancouver is looking for ways to increase density by, as Croll says, encouraging the "transferring of density from our other land holdings into the Cypress Village area to concentrate density close to the new services and preserve even more green space in other parts of the municipality." While this will "use up available development potential and limit development on our undeveloped land . . . there will likely be more homes and therefore more residents as we make the homes smaller and keep the buildable floor area constant."

The citizens of West Vancouver will soon debate which vision will frame much of their future, and that of their children and grandchildren (and how they will ever be able to afford it). An outline of a planning process for Cypress Village went to council in April 2016, and in December 2017 council approved moving forward with the "pre-conditions" phase of this process. There is still much planning and public input to come, including a review by a Cypress Village Working Group. Croll sees this as a twenty-year plan. BPP has been committed to West Vancouver now for over eighty years, and will continue its interactions with the community for decades to come.

> The slowest burning candles in the world, altar carvings fashioned from a single piece of wood, a beauty shop where individuality is more important than fads and fashions, are some of the fascinations I found in West Vancouver shops.
>
> —Jean Jones, *"In West Vancouver"* (pamphlet)

Catering to the affluent women of West Vancouver, Eaton's opened the Regent Room in the women's department in 1962, where customers could try on the latest fur-trimmed coats.

West Vancouver Museum and Archives, 62.060.WVA. BPP, Val Tkatschow photo

05

COMMERCIAL VENTURES

Park Royal Mall

In earlier days, most commercial activity focused on Marine Drive with stores in Ambleside and Dundarave developing in a natural and more or less organic fashion to serve the needs of the locals. These still play a significant role in the community, but as West Vancouver has grown, Park Royal has taken centre stage, both a result and driver of the residential community.

British developers scuttled BPP's initial plans for a shopping centre at the top of Taylor Way when some of them thought to take a closer look at the rugged topography. The flat land farther down the hill that became Park Royal, which opened in 1950, offered a more benign space on which to build. Caulfeild Shopping Centre, which opened in 1987 on the southern fringes of BPP's western land holdings, provided additional commercial space. Cypress Village, the properties' proposed showpiece on the western end of the development, will accommodate the population density to support a variety of commercial and cultural amenities (see chapter 4).

Malls are in many ways natural extensions of car culture, playing key roles in modern communities, especially in suburban areas where driving and shopping are interwoven threads in the cultural fabric. Along with television and fast food, malls helped define some of the nature of modern middle-class life after the Second World War, developing as large numbers of young married couples moved to the suburbs for affordable housing. Malls now offer a one-stop venue where every family member can find much to fill their needs and wishes. Young people hang out at malls after (sometimes during) school, while older folks might enjoy a combination of shopping and lunch, or perhaps a beer at a local pub or a specialty coffee at a cozy bistro.

Although Park Royal has often been credited with being the first shopping centre in Canada, that position properly belongs to Norgate Shopping Centre, which opened in 1949 in the Montreal suburb of Ville de Saint-Laurent. Many American centres also preceded Park Royal, particularly Seattle's Northgate.[64] However, Park Royal was the first mall in Canada to be anchored by a department store (Woodward's) and one of the few regional shopping centres in Canada that has been privately owned since its inception, which gives the management greater

By 1937 the developers realized they would have to include some necessities of life for the occupants of the British Properties. Accordingly, the Olmsted brothers produced a plan for a small shopping centre and filling station straddling the corner of 7th Street (now Taylor Way) and Marine Drive. *Courtesy of the National Park Service, Frederick Law Olmsted National Historic Site*

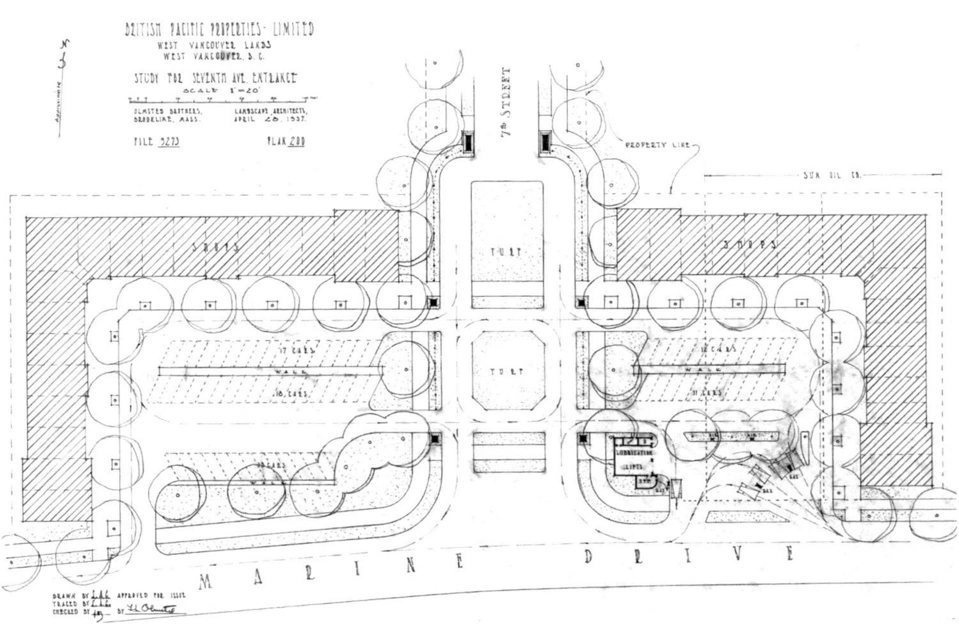

control over its direction. In an almost symbiotic relationship with West Vancouver and the British Properties, Park Royal has grown from a modest strip of stores north of Marine Drive to a complex upscale development reflecting the wishes of an affluent market. Expansions and redirections every few years have kept it current with the changing nature of modern shopping malls.

First Steps

In the 1930s, the Guinness Company built London's Park Royal Brewery, from which Park Royal Shopping Centre inherited its name. Financed by the sale of the British Properties' building lots, the mall at the north-west corner of Marine Drive and Taylor Way sought to lure prospective residents (particularly wives?) to live in the new development.

On August 2, 1961, suited representatives of Eaton's surround Chief Mathias Joe of the Squamish First Nation at the sod turning for the development of Park Royal South. *West Vancouver Museum and Archives, 61.109.WVA.BPP*

Guinness representative P.D. (Perry) Willoughby worked out plans with W.C. Woodward for the $1.5-million centre. Architect C.B.K. Van Norman designed the structure and Willoughby became its first manager. Woodward turned the sod in August 1949 while Willoughby, Chief Mathias Joe and others looked on. (At least three chiefs have carried the names Joe Mathias or Mathias Joe; this Mathias Joe is distinct from both Chief Mathias Joe/Joe Capilano and his great-grandson Chief Joe Mathias.) The mall opened almost exactly a year later, on September 1, 1950, with 125,000 square feet of retail space and parking for 750 cars. In 1955, after Willoughby passed away, Edward Richardson, who had joined BPP in 1948, succeeded him as manager, soon incorporating his own idea for open planted areas.

Ideally located to siphon customers from busy Marine Drive, Park

On September 1, 1950, the Woodward's department store opened in Park Royal. Mr. Woodward (centre) was there to greet the first customers. *Vancouver Public Library, Special Collections, VPL.81408C, Artray photo studio*

Park Royal, with its prodigious parking lot, was founded on the automobile way of life. It was natural, then, to open a gas station on the same day that Woodward's opened ushering in a new way of shopping for the car-going public. The Standard station held this site for more than three decades. *Vancouver Public Library, Special Collections, VPL.81407D, Artray studios*

Royal also attracted visitors from Vancouver, who could take the scenic drive through Stanley Park and over the new bridge at a time when more benign traffic made this an attractive option. In the early years, shoppers accessed the strip of shops from outside, in many ways not hugely different from the way they accessed the walk-by shopping in Ambleside and Dundarave, although the mall offered the convenience of free off-street parking. Columnist Myra Moir reported enthusiastically at its opening that the "curtain rose today on the smartest shopping centre in Canada. . . . The centre will make North Shore shoppers the most pampered shoppers in the Dominion." Designed with "scarlet geraniums set on gardens along the sidewalks, a musical background and a marble fountain,"[65] the mall also included the latest in dazzling modern innovations: magic eyes to open doors, shopping carts (ideal for transporting young children) and turntable grocery checkouts. Francis Lovegrove of the *West Vancouver News* enthused: "The whole array of buildings are of strictly modern design in which the straight line is dominant, but so changed by variations in construction of the company units and in the interior lighting and set-up of those as to do away with the monotony that might have been expected."[66]

Many of the larger Vancouver stores had turned down offers to set up a branch in the wilds of the North Shore. Woodward's, an exception, anchored the mall at one end—a bold step at the time for a major store to venture away from the security of the urban core. Its venture paid off. It added a second floor in 1953, and in 1961 opened a 30,000-square-foot "supermarket" food floor. Woolworth's also took a chance, opening its first branch outside downtown. Twenty other businesses included a medical centre, clothing store, drugstore, gas station and beauty salon. "Merchandise from the four quarters of the globe" came to West Vancouver. As most stores were independently operated, they could supply goods not generally available at chain stores in Vancouver. Many targeted an upscale clientele, but the presence of Woolworth's and Woodward's assured the average family that they, too, could buy their necessities here, and do so affordably.

With initial business slow, skeptics wondered how this ambitious development could ever attain economic viability: Who would trek across that new bridge to shop in West Vancouver when downtown Vancouver provided all one could want? George McDonald, owner of Kennedy-McDonald clothing, recalled that his store was open three

A French-style sidewalk café in Park Royal, Maurice's was the upscale place to dine on a day of shopping. *West Vancouver Museum and Archives, 0193.WVA.DOC*

days before he had his first cash sale—a $5 tie. But although it took the shopping centre about four years to attract the needed customers, the risk takers eventually reaped their rewards. In 1975, ten of the original smaller businesses were still operating, including Ena Swires's linen shop, Dorothy Watson's Charmante Gowns, Doug Alderson's Fine Arts Shop, George Beveridge's The Nut House, Archer Holden's Capilano Hobbies and the Standard Oil station, managed by Bob Nelson.

Growing prosperity after the war gave many a greater disposable income, with shopping centres catering to the burgeoning middle class. As Vancouver emerged from its small city roots, Park Royal incorporated elements of the larger world. Many discovered it as a place where shopping met lifestyle. Some enjoyed Maurice's sidewalk café, where the new sophisticates could sample French cuisine, including snails and frog legs, dishes such as Mille Feuilles Bourguignon, or one of twenty-five varieties of French omelette. The brick fireplace had a cheery log fire; on rainy winter days, with maple tables, rush-bottomed chairs, beamed ceilings and coral-coloured walls, it provided an attractive ambience.

Black Ball Ferries' Sunshine Coast service, which opened August 11, 1951, with the *Bainbridge* and the *Quillayute,* brought in customers from the growing communities of Gibsons and points north on the Sunshine Coast. These car ferries made it possible, for the first time, for residents

By 1965, traffic jams were common at the corner of Taylor Way and Marine Drive. The gateway to West Van was guarded on the left by the White Spot, and on the right by the Standard gas station. *West Vancouver Museum and Archives, 0080.WVA.HAR*

of the Sunshine Coast, Nanaimo and elsewhere, to have a day's family outing while shopping in a full-service mall. Commuters to Vancouver also found it convenient; some parked their cars at the mall while busing to their workplaces across the Lions Gate Bridge. Development ventured south of Marine Drive with the 1955 opening of White Spot (not on Squamish land), a drive-in venue for seventy-four cars combined with indoor lunch counters.

The success of the North Mall encouraged further expansion on the south side of Marine Drive on sixty-seven acres leased from the Squamish, who agreed to move twelve homes to accommodate the shopping centre. Chief Joe Mathias lived approximately where The Keg now stands.

The South Mall

BPP president Peter Finch and architect Peter Blewett toured over forty North American shopping centres to prepare for the South Mall. The $7-million project opened October 3, 1962, the peaks on its roof intended to echo the North Shore mountains. Super Valu and Eaton's anchored the addition, with thirty-four other shops providing a varied shopping experience.

The large interior concourse of the South Mall enabled all-season entertainment for shoppers, including this well-attended fashion show in the 1970s. *West Vancouver Museum and Archives, 70S.008.WVA.BPP. Jack Lindsay photo*

Many of the local citizenry remained as wary of Park Royal's success as some had previously been of its potential failure, especially objecting to plans for dreaded apartment towers. The Park Royal Towers to the northwest of the mall, considered an integral part of the mall development and an extension of the new waterfront apartments, had been on the books from 1959. Built on Squamish land and completed in 1965, these three seventeen-storey towers were among the larger apartment buildings in West Vancouver at this time, with one-bedrooms renting from $125 a month.

Especially in its early years, Park Royal cultivated community connections. The common space of the South Mall provided an ideal location for fashion shows, art exhibits, boat shows, choirs and even a symphony. Visiting attractions included the Purcell Quartet, the Vancouver Symphony and a Japanese wood-block artist, among many others. Super Valu's palomino horse ride at a dime a go proved a great attraction for children, while Easter egg hunts, dog shows and costume contests helped integrate Park Royal into the community. Eventually the

No object was too large for display inside the mall in Park Royal. Although not a regular consumer item, this small plane was nonetheless an attraction to customers. *West Vancouver Museum and Archives, 60S.033.WVA.BPP. Per Rasmussen photo*

A swirl of activity, this Kinsmen Regatta square dance night, full of dancing teenagers and adults, was one of many community events that were part of life in Park Royal in the 1950s. *West Vancouver Museum and Archives, 51.022.WVA.BPP*

palominos went out of commission, but in 1995 Park Royal butcher Peter Black and his wife Helen refurbished them and for a time the children could ride again. Odeon's cinemas opened in 1967 in the South Mall, the only ones west of Toronto in a shopping complex. Other entertainment options included a bowling alley with thirty-six lanes and ten billiard tables. With something for virtually everyone, the mall often enjoyed 25,000 visitors on a Saturday.

Other stores catered to the new sophistication that higher disposable incomes made possible. Edward Neubauer's Spanish Village specialized in design that was "artistically correct in balance, scale, unity," such as "light fixtures from Spain and Mexico, accessories like pewter, silver, brass from all over the world besides the furniture, half of which is English and imported from England, and the other half Spanish, imported from Spain."

North Mall Expansion

In 1969, architect Peter Blewett, with designers Brian Cranfield and Colin Stephens, enclosed the North Mall, using natural materials to create a rich, warm environment. The $7 million project created the feel of a "log cabin in winter," according to North Shore journalist Noel Wright, a departure from the antiseptic look of most malls at the time.

Many of Park Royal's challenges rose from having, in effect, two malls separated by a six-lane street. Attempts to integrate the two included an overpass that allowed cars to move back and forth, a street-level light so pedestrians could cross Marine Drive, and a five-cent, twelve-passenger commuter bus between Park Royal Towers and the two malls. The commuter bus began service February 4, 1970, and lasted until 1996, when the $100,000 yearly cost forced its closure. A planned gondola connecting the two malls was never built.

As the years went by, many of the stores reflected cultural and lifestyle change. By 1975, plants at Woolworth's had become a big seller, going for "as high as $80 and our best customers are young people." By the same year, Charmante's fashion wear store had moved once and expanded three times. "We have a loyal following of customers who, even if they move from the North Shore, return to shop at Charmante's," said proprietor Dorothy Watson. Linen shop owner Ena Swires noted the change in colours of linen from "white, or ecru. Or possibly pastel. But new synthetics in bright, vivid colours that can be mixed or matched are the main sellers," adding that "materials have changed, because young women won't iron." Doug Alderson's specialty in Inuit (then called Eskimo) sculptures became so successful that it split off into a new establishment, the Park Gallery.

An elegant classical sculpture in Carrera marble, titled *Muse and Her Playful Cherubim* and depicting a lute-playing muse surrounded by four cherubim, had been originally owned by John D. Rockefeller. Noted

The peripatetic Salieres sculpture looks out over a kiddies' amusement park set up in Park Royal in July 1951. The sculpture, which cost about $19,000 when it was created for a Cornelius Billings estate in New York some time between 1905 and 1910, was purchased by John D. Rockefeller, Jr. (along with the estate) in 1917. Around 1936, Rockefeller in turn either sold or gave the sculpture group to Lord Southborough, a British Properties investor, presumably for the grand entrance park at the top of Taylor Way. It was moved to the south side in the '80s, and now languishes in a container in the municipal works yard. *West Vancouver Museum and Archives, 51.010.WVA.BPP. Eric Cable photo*

French sculptor Sylvain Salieres based it on a design by noted art dealer P.W. French. In 1936, then owner Lord Southborough moved it from its location on the Billings Estate in New York and donated it to the British Properties. No suitable location could be found within the properties, so it was moved to Park Royal North when it opened in 1950, where it remained until 1962, when it was relocated to a spot near Woodward's food floor in Park Royal South. It was again relegated to storage in 1969 but found a new home in a pool outside the skylight mall between Eaton's and Super Valu in the South Mall in 1977. Current art at Park Royal focuses on Indigenous art.

South Mall Expansion

The first studies for the expansion of the South Mall were carried out in 1968. Beginning about 1971, plans for its major expansion brought Park Royal, the municipality and the Squamish Nation into some intense debate. Although the 1970 Peace Arch decision had confirmed the rights of Indigenous people to control the land on their reserves, the municipality made known its reluctance to accept that position. In 1975 Mayor Peter Jones sought assurances that further Park Royal development would not take place without the approval of the West Vancouver council, indicating that he'd go to court if traffic, parkland, economic and aesthetic safeguards were not assured.

In fact, neither the municipal government nor the ratepayers' groups had any legal avenue for preventing this development, and both the Squamish and the municipality realized that with the shopping centre paying over a million dollars yearly in taxes and employing over 2,500 people, municipal opposition would only go so far. The centre was here to stay. Chief Philip Joe commented, "If we wanted to make a fast buck, we would have put up hot dog stands and service stations."

Swedish Jeweler, in Park Royal since 1966, moved to larger premises after the 1978 expansion. Their designs incorporate fine gemstones—diamonds from South Africa, rubies and sapphires from Thailand, star sapphires from Ceylon, opals from Australia and pearls from Japan and the South Seas.

—The *Citizen*, August 2, 1978

On August 1, 1978, the 2nd Baron Moyne, accompanied by his grandson, and joined by Khot-la-Cha, Chief Simon Baker of the Squamish band, unveiled a plaque identifying the "Dairmid Guinness" bridge. Now referred to as the Wardance Bridge, spanning the Capilano and leading to the Squamish reserve, it was originally named in memory of Dairmid, Lord Moyne's son, who had died of cancer the previous year. His presence shows the ongoing connection between the Guinness family, the British Properties and the Squamish. *West Vancouver Museum and Archives, 78.109.WVA.BPP. Jack Lindsay photo*

More vigorous opposition came from the West Vancouver Ratepayers, a coalition of nine ratepayers' and citizens' groups whose main concern was traffic, especially the growing traffic tangle at Marine Drive and Taylor Way. Perhaps they had the possible effect of the major residential development planned on Squamish land in the back of their minds, but most of that did not take place. A bridge across the Capilano to North Vancouver relieved some of the traffic pressure, but traffic remains a significant problem.

The $22-million South Mall expansion, opened August 2, 1978, added numerous new stores, more than doubling its shopping space to 500,000 square feet. Aiming for a complete cross-section of the best downtown stores with a mix of local, regional and national stores to provide an interesting variety for shoppers, the project took a decidedly upscale direction. In 1984 alone five new stores opened, geared exclusively to women's fashion. Other new businesses included a specialty liquor store with 150 varieties of imported wine, and electronics stores to usher West Vancouver into the Information Age.

An open court provided a place to mingle and shop beside reflecting pools, a fountain and tropical greenery under a light, airy pyramid roof; it was "like stepping out into the garden on a sunny spring day," Noel Wright enthused in the *North Shore News*. Architect Peter Blewett developed a unique identity, and the Wintergarden food fair provided the sensation of eating outdoors, with an international menu in a garden-like setting.

> Hand-loomed silks from Thailand provide a riot of colour, and Oriental knits give promise of glamorous entrances to after-five parties. Jewellery pieces are conversation pieces, especially a pair of black-sequin earrings I spotted that must be the largest danglers in the country. There are beaded purses, sequinned evening shoes, and adorable teak figures, trays and salad bowls. Here is where I found those fabulous altar carvings, actually religious works of art from Taoist temples.[67]

This expansion made Park Royal the largest shopping centre west of Toronto, which in 1978 brought in $1.3 million annually to municipal coffers while using only $40,000 worth of municipal services and employing four thousand people. It also made Park Royal the first shopping centre to attract all three of Canada's top department stores: Hudson's Bay, Eaton's and Woodward's.

Not entirely satisfied with the direction of development, Mayor Jones wanted something a little more than some nice shops, hoping for "social and cultural facilities normally associated with such a large development." A number of events held in the 1980s partially addressed this need. In 1981 the Vancouver Symphony Orchestra held twenty-nine concerts in the North Mall while Vancouver's Orpheum Theatre shut its doors due to labour problems. In 1986 Britain's Guildhall String Ensemble played. But generally this has become, like most malls today, a place to shop rather than a community centre for entertainment and social interaction. The focus for community activity has shifted west and is now amply filled by the huge and well-equipped community centres in Ambleside/Dundarave and Gleneagles, as well as cultural offerings in the Ferry Building, the Silk Purse, the Kay Meek Centre and at summer festivals. Current Park Royal community liaison Rick Amantea plans to change this, making the mall a place for more active socializing and entertainment.

Mary Swain ran the popular Royal Seafoods from 1961 to 1990. "[A] touch of dill, a breath of garlic and a speck of mayonnaise is all the help fresh fish needs."

The North Shore and beyond, including Squamish and Whistler, have become favourite year-round playgrounds, and Horseshoe Bay is a destination for those taking the ferries, which makes central West Vancouver less of a destination. The 1946 Bartholomew report had suggested that "from the Capilano River Bridge to 13th Street it is recommended that an imposing parkway entrance, 120 feet (36 metres) wide, be constructed" to give West Vancouver definition. This didn't happen. Perhaps because of its immersion in a growing metropolis, West Vancouver's identity has become more nebulous.

Purchase and Development by Larco

In 1990 the Guinness family put Park Royal up for sale, including the bowling alley, theatres and the Kapilano office building just to the east. Thirteen companies bid, with Larco successful at an estimated $160 million, much of which BPP channelled into their new residential developments in the Upper Lands. Larco, whose principals are North Shore residents, with new managers Amin and Shiraz Lalji, soon developed plans for change and expansion. In the mid-'80s renovation in shopping malls emphasized a bright, upscale look; Park Royal had not kept up. Like most shopping centres it has never been, at least on the outside, an aesthetic delight. The new owners wanted to appeal to a younger demographic, with space for community meetings, group activities and business functions.

Unfortunately, in 1993 Larco displayed a monumental misunderstanding of the West Vancouver community by bulldozing four acres of forest south of Park Royal for a driving range, complete with high wattage lights to keep the mostly elderly neighbours awake. In West Vancouver councillor Alan Williams's words, they showed "an incredible lack of vision."

Bernie Smith, a retired policeman turned Park Royal security guard, delighted customers with his constant and melodious whistling. He could make his whistle warble and flutter between notes like a bird call.

Plans for some new big-box stores encountered strong community opposition. The Coalition for a Healthy Community gathered more than 15,000 signatures opposing what they saw as insensitive development. *Vancouver Sun* columnist Denny Boyd expressed the view of many: "One hell of a lot of us don't like it, don't want it, really have no use for it." Some bystanders, who were perhaps more objective, pointed out that many of the local businessmen expressing adamant opposition to the development were likely involved in various similar projects on the other side of the Lions Gate Bridge. In 1997 Larco unveiled plans, which included three big-box stores—Home Depot, Toys"R"Us and PetSmart—to intense and prolonged public outcry. A public meeting of four hundred at West Vancouver Secondary School was one of several such gatherings in which residents voiced strenuous objections, ultimately forcing Larco to drastically modify its plans.

This was one of the times when the conservative opposition to development got it right. Park Royal agreed that future plans would include dialogue with the West Vancouver council, providing opportunity for community input.

Shannon Humphrey weighed in with a delightfully tongue-in-cheek article in the *North Shore News,* channelling the wishes of the iconic West Vancouver housewife, who "usually has blond streaks in her hair, big diamond rings on her fingers, large, firm breasts despite childbearing, a fit physique which is the result of hours spent with a handsome personal trainer, and a wardrobe full of athletic looking clothes." Forget Home Depot, she said; no one in West Van does home repair. Replace it with something like a Plastic Surgery Depot. Replace Toys"R"Us with Boys"R"Us, a source of renovation specialists. PetSmart? Why not a Mutual Fund Mart?

Eventually Larco yielded, although, as the mall was on Squamish land, the municipality could not refuse permission to build. Larco returned in 2003 with plans for smaller stores in a more user-friendly development and the Home Depot reduced from 120,000 to a still sizable 70,000 square feet with a "boutique-like set-up." At least the store didn't look boxy; apparently aesthetics compensates for size, although Shoppers Drug Mart emerged a few years later with a box-like profile that has escaped public outcry.

The new development opened in 2004 as The Village on the west end of the mall; anchored by Whole Foods and Home Depot, it aimed to re-create the feel of main street shopping (as in Ambleside and Dundarave). Designed by Vancouver-based architects Musson Cattell Mackey Partnership working with F&A Architecture of California, it comprises eight separate buildings with diverse architectural styles and exteriors. Larger stores, such as Home Sense, Whole Foods and Home Depot, balance smaller ones, many of which have a clothing and fashion orientation, some identified only by their corporate logos. The Village Taphouse is crowned with the facsimile of a lighthouse; a Tesla showroom and a variety of stylish bistros for people-watching as much as eating reflect the ambience of a community that prides itself on being current. The development has found favour with most, receiving the 2006 International Design and Development Award from the International Council of Shopping Centers. Meanwhile Larco continues to expand its empire, buying nine federal properties in 2007 and recently acquiring Ottawa's iconic Fairmont Château Laurier hotel.

So the shopping centre has come full circle, back in some ways to the open model it started with in 1950. The Village was Canada's first lifestyle centre, catering to an older, sophisticated, cultured audience. As community liaison Rick Amantea said, "You won't see many skateboarding stores"—earlier plans of catering to a younger audience were derailed by West Vancouver's aging population, who are not generally ardent skateboarders, and also, no doubt, have a higher disposable income.

Local entertainment opportunities remain slim. The Odeon theatre closed in 1990 and Park Royal theatres in 2000, leaving no movie theatres in West Vancouver. The bowling alley met the wrecker's ball in 2003 and the driving range closed January 31, 2003. But gradually leisure activities are reviving. Plans exist for an eleven-theatre Cineplex at Park Royal, to be built over the Sports Shack and Brick stores. Meanwhile, over in Ambleside, the Kay Meek Centre opened November 6, 2004, the day that its generous patron Kay Meek died. The Grosvenor Theatre and Studio Theatre now offer a variety of musical, theatrical and public events, including a film series, and will join forces with the Grosvenor development in entertainment offerings.

Full circle. The current popular outdoor gathering places of Park Royal South hark back to the original Park Royal North of the 1950s. *Photo by John Moir*

New retailers continue to appear at Park Royal, with many reflecting the more eclectic tastes of an increasingly multicultural community. In 2010, T&T opened the Osaka supermarket specializing in Asian food, with sixty kinds of miso and eighty types of Japanese noodles for the growing number of Asian residents and others who are developing a taste for international and fusion cuisines. An international food fair has opened on the second floor of the South Mall. A new fashion wing anchored by Simons extends the availability of upscale fashions, especially for women. Over two hundred shops make Park Royal Vancouver's second-largest shopping centre; it currently grosses $650 million annually. However, while it continues to provide employment for many, most employees live outside West Vancouver, where they can find affordable accommodation.

Although the mall is on Squamish land, very little inside Park Royal—stores, employees or customers—reflects its Indigenous location. Local artist Jody Broomfield has created the *Salmon Spindle Whorl* to pay homage to the Squamish women weavers who used the spinning tool. Ray Naratrora's nearby *Thunderbird* sculpture gives the Squamish a small cultural presence more in tune with its environment than the elegant European fountain that graced the mall in earlier times. But more could be done to remind shoppers and residents of the Indigenous people whose culture is rooted deeply in the past.

The North Mall Expands—Future Plans

On July 24, 2014, council approved a series of changes to the North Mall, including the elimination of the interior mall. Larger stores with a more regional orientation have generally replaced the smaller boutique-style stores. Major tenants, which now include Loblaw's City Market, Saks off 5th, Hudson's Bay, Banana Republic, the Gap, Talbots, a huge liquor store and the Steve Nash Park Royal Sports Club satisfy a wide range of the community's needs. These complement developments on the south side, which include more restaurants and fashion. A new exterior façade harmonizes the north and south sides; with the new shops on the South Mall, this creates a feeling of closeness between the two. In a return to the mall's roots, shoppers can now access nearly half the space in the mall from the outside.

Besides the new theatre complex, plans include two mid-rise apartment buildings of no more than fourteen storeys on the old White Spot site. Although this won't be on Squamish land, adjacent amenities such as a restaurant will be, requiring close cooperation between Park Royal management and the Squamish Nation. Rick Amantea hopes construction will start in 2018 and finish in the spring of 2021, but at the time of writing these buildings had not yet received municipal approval.

Amantea, who has worked for Park Royal since 1991, was hired in 2013 as the vice-president for Community Partnerships and Development. His vision for the mall over the next five to thirty years is of an environment that combines commercial, office, recreation, leisure and residential space. It will, he says, be a place where people can shop, live and play, including a brand new community gathering place. Although emphasis has generally been on commercial aspects, he says the intent in the past six years has been to make Park Royal more of a community within the larger community of West Vancouver. Eight kilometres of walkable routes and four kilometres of bike lanes foster a more environmentally conscious atmosphere.

Caulfeild Shopping Centre

Most of West Vancouver is a long drive from Park Royal, and most of the municipality's recent growth has been in the western communities, where shops are few. Beginning in 1976, development in Caulfeild Plateau added 810 units, or about 2,000 new residents, to the 2,700 already living in that area, making a place to buy life's necessities (and perhaps a few luxuries) essential. Don Milliken of Daon Developments recalls many meetings with Peter Finch, British Properties manager, where they discussed its configuration. Daon wanted a larger centre, but agreed to limit the supermarket to 25,000 square feet, at least 10,000 square feet smaller than they preferred.

Bell Enterprise Development Centre acquired 5.3 acres of BPP land just south of the highway for what it billed as a neighbourhood shopping centre including a supermarket gourmet store by Safeway. Called Someplace Special, it became the first of its kind in Canada, offering, among other things, seventy-two varieties of mustard to titillate every palate. Architects Ernie and Grace Collins, who had experience designing homes in West Vancouver, helped to create a residential feel for the mall. Pharmasave, BC Liquor Stores, the Bank of Montreal and Starbucks came on board as major tenants.

A much smaller centre than Park Royal, costing $10 million and occupying 69,000 square feet, Caulfeild offers a more traditional sidewalk-and-parking-lot configuration, with stores accessed from the outside. But thirty stores were enough to stir the ire of many in the community, some of whom feared "it was not for the convenience of locals." Key to their objection was the quiet increase of the allotted land from 3.15 to 5.3 acres, probably a simple matter of topography: the commercial zoning was set at Timberfield Road, but when the road actually went in it swung wide, adding an extra 1.5 acres. This was used as a green belt to serve as a buffer for the neighbours.

This increased size, however, became a politically divisive issue. Former mayor Don Lanskail complained that "the area designated was intended to be a relatively small shopping centre for the convenience of the people living there." Many feared that traffic or other ills would compromise the peaceful harmony of their lives, while Dundarave merchants expressed concern about losing business. In June 1985, 175 Caulfeild residents signed a petition asking the municipal council to reject the shopping centre proposal. Resident Lee Broderick regretted that "we improve the tax base at the expense of the people."

Mayor Derrick Humphreys supported the project, believing that the existing land-use contract should be recognized.[68] Others strongly opposed it and eighteen irate petitioners took the case to BC's Supreme Court to block development. Russel Precious of the Merchants of Dundarave Association argued that the 1978 land-use contract had specified zoning for small (rather than large) commercial use for the Caulfeild commercial area. Opposition proved unsuccessful and the project proceeded.

In an ironic twist, in the 1986 municipal election, shopping centre critic Don Lanskail ousted Humphreys as mayor, so a smiling Lanskail cut the ribbon at the official opening in October 1987. Since then, the centre has developed into a valued part of the community. Don Milliken recalls meeting some of the objectors as they enjoyed the mall on opening day. People now shop and socialize here, often meeting up with their friends in Starbucks for a social coffee. It definitely has a community feel.

The preservation of 15 per cent of the plateau in its natural state has created an environment that most residents now accept and appreciate. One can only imagine the roars of outrage if the shopping centre closed and the local residents had to trek to Park Royal to buy their basic needs and savour their cappuccinos and conversation. The relatively small parking lot provides a convenient setting for many community events that enhance the quality of life in this area.

> Let us build houses that restore to man the life-giving, life-enhancing elements of nature . . . in the rightness of a house on the land, we sense fitness we call beauty.
>
> —Architect Joseph A. Barry

This 1974 house in Lions Bay showed how innovative architecture could merge buildings with terrain that had been previously considered unbuildable. Architect: Barry Griblin.

Drawing courtesy of the architect

06

MODERNIST ARCHITECTURE

TRANSFORMING SPACES INTO PLACES

The early development of the British Properties coincided closely with the development of modernist architecture in Canada. After the Second World War some brilliant architectural minds transformed much of the geography of West Vancouver, particularly parts of the properties, into stunning homes. A booming economy didn't hurt.

Prior to the Second World War, architecture in West Vancouver ran the gamut from Cotswold cottages to the *moderne* style. Where they leaned on local models and abundant lumber from the local forests, the results were mostly functional log cabins and simple wood frame dwellings that harmonized with the landscape. Many of the Hollyburn ski cabins are splendid examples of what ingenuity can do with simple local materials. Like the modernist houses built farther down the slope, they created spaces in which people could be attuned to the rhythms of surrounding nature.

The *moderne* style, a precursor to modernism, developed from the 1920s, employing geometric designs with softened angles and sweeping curved corners, horizontal balustrades and flat roofs. The plain white exterior surfaces were generally finished with smooth white stucco or concrete. Square or rectangular windows may follow the curvature of the building; small glass panes or glass blocks can add interior lighting and exterior design. Echoing ocean liners with railings, decks and canopies, the structures riffed on the romance of ocean travel. West Vancouver examples include the Bennett House at 2909 Mathers Avenue (1937) and the Langley House at 1660 29th Street (1938), both designed by H.C. Berchtenbreiter.

The modernist movement in architecture paralleled a transformation in the other arts at the beginning of the twentieth century. Modernism affected every aspect of Western culture, reacting to the fussy detail in late Victorian art, opting instead for a clean and hard look and feel. In literature, it eschewed lush Victorian verse for the rugged topography of T.S. Eliot and Ezra Pound. In music, Igor Stravinsky's *The Rites of Spring* (1913) incorporated new forms of tonality, rhythm and dissonance. The devastation of the First World War accelerated the change, demanding that artists confront the world in new ways and incorporate a harsher reality in their work.

In architecture, the new international style emphasized innovations that industrial materials and new technology allowed while facilitating the use of geometric forms that transcended national boundaries, basing buildings on structure and function rather than ornamentation. European architecture used steel and concrete to achieve this end, but North Americans felt more at home with wood, stone and other local building materials.

Viennese émigré architects Rudolf Schindler and Richard Neutra arrived in California in the early 1920s. Neutra, who had worked briefly with Frank Lloyd Wright, developed "a humanistic architecture in response to place." Neutra became celebrated for "rigorously geometric but airy structures," his work blending art, landscape and practical comfort. "With their sliding glass walls and carefully considered relationship with nature, these houses connected the world of Japanese Zen Buddhism to the great American outdoors."[69] Positioned on the Pacific Rim between Europe and Asia, the West Coast drew on both European and Asian traditions. Japan and Canada shared a mutual dependence on wood, and many Canadian modernists were influenced by the Japanese aesthetic of harmonious diversity and connection to nature, with low silhouettes, fine wood detailing and roof shapes. They always incorporated a water feature and gardens figured prominently.

The Lower Mainland in the 1940s still functioned in relative isolation from the larger centres in eastern North America and Europe, depending

By the late 1950s and '60s academic theories of modernism made their way into the mainstream in West Vancouver, often the butt of jokes by popular local satirists. Seen here on his deck, *Vancouver Sun* cartoonist Len Norris was well known for his gentle jibes at the highbrow West Van mountainside lifestyle. His choice of house? A stylish modernist design high on a hill in West Vancouver with a commanding view of English Bay. *Library and Archives Canada/National Film Board of Canada fonds/e011176821*

for much of its cultural inspiration on California. Neutra visited Vancouver in 1946 and 1953 to lecture at the newly created UBC School of Architecture, holding two salons at the home of B.C. (Bert) Binning, who'd built one of the first (and still surviving) modernist homes in West Vancouver, on Mathers in Altamont. Neutra's views—that cities should be built according to technological principles, and design can shape our lives in maximizing the possibilities of human fulfillment—echo those of Ebenezer Howard. Aesthetics can change the way we think, the way we interact with other people. As Steve Jobs later often said, "Design is not so much how it looks as how it works." Neutra inspired Arthur Erickson, Ron Thom and other influential modernist voices in the next generation of architects.

The longest surviving architectural firm in Vancouver was founded by George Lister Thornton Sharp and Charles Joseph Thompson in 1908. Ned Pratt, a larger-than-life figure who loved Shakespeare and won a bronze medal in the double sculls at the 1932 Olympics, joined the firm in 1937, as did Bob Berwick. They became partners in 1945, shifting the firm toward the principles of modernism. The apprenticeships of

Built in 1939, the Thornton house in Caulfeild, with its two-storey post-and-beam construction and proudly exposed skeletal framework, represented a modernist break with traditional design and building practices. Meticulously renovated and maintained, it stands today as a testament to the enduring value of intelligent design.
Photo by John Moir

Ron Thom and Fred Hollingsworth here in the late 1940s assured the company's ascendance in the West Coast modernist architectural world.

Hollingsworth designed the neoteric house, using fir beams and inexpensive cedar panelling to create a house that provided an open, livable space, which could easily be replicated and adapted to the needs of different clients. He built about fourteen, some of them still providing pleasant living spaces today. In 1963 he formed a loose association with like-minded architects, including Bud Wood, Beans Justice, Arthur Erickson and Barry Downs, whose synergy produced some of the best West Coast residential architecture of the mid-century. "Thompson, Berwick & Pratt became a beacon for aspiring modernists on the West Coast, and the largest graduate school in Canada."[70]

Architect Peter Thornton built one of the earliest modernist houses for himself and his mother in 1939 at 4785 Piccadilly South in the heart of Lower Caulfeild. Thornton had graduated from the Architectural Association School of Architecture in London, England, where he had been exposed to the work of Marcel Breuer and Walter Gropius. The house on Piccadilly, adapted from his student project, featured one of the first flat roofs in West Vancouver. At this time, CMHC would not approve mortgages for flat-roofed houses, although this was for aesthetic rather than structural reasons (many larger buildings had flat roofs). Flat roofs made it easier to build four- to five-foot (1.2–1.5-metre) overhangs, which provided protection from rainy days and the summer sun and allowed the house plan to adapt to uneven terrain. It also facilitated integration with the natural environment.

B.C. Binning's house is one of modernism's iconic achievements. An artist rather than an architect, he had studied under Group of Seven artists Fred Varley and Jock Macdonald, and English sculptor Henry Moore, and during a two-year stay in Europe had also studied the new work of European architects. He built his 1,400-square-foot home in 1941 on Mathers Crescent in Altamont with assistance from architects Pratt and Berwick. Reached through a terraced garden, his home's southern exposure, facing away from the street, follows the slopes of the lot. The south wall is mostly glazed with floor-to-ceiling glass, and a flat roof and clerestory windows let light in. "As Bert's wife Jessie said, "the house was an attempt to show what you could do when you didn't have a lot of money, but had imagination."[71]

In 1997 the Binning House was designated a National Historic Site,

Looking weary of all the forces at work both for and against it, the decaying Binning House waits for a permanent resolution. Heritage home preservation is an ongoing challenge in West Van. *Photo by John Moir*

and in 1999 a Municipal Heritage Site. Unfortunately the relentless rains of the West Coast have not been kind to it and evidence of rot means it will require extensive (and expensive) repairs for its survival. Plans outlining the enhanced protection and complete restoration have been detailed in a Heritage Revitalization Agreement (HRA) submitted to the district. Long-term goals in the agreement include that it will become a private museum. Key to the plan is the division of the property into two lots, with an infill house built on the lower lot, with the sloping lot ensuring that the ocean view from the Binning House will be retained. Sale of the infill house will finance the restoration work. These plans were still, as of early 2018, in the discussion stage, but if successful will save the life of an architectural icon.

Driven by a deep connection to landscape, modernist architecture blurs boundaries between inner and outer worlds, making for cleaner, more livable spaces. In Thom's words, "a building has to make love to a site." The landscape itself acquired significance often equal to the house

Building for a coastal landscape.

Looking toward Lighthouse Park.
Photo by John Moir

For over 100 years, the mountainside terrain of West Vancouver has attracted dreamers and designers, both amateur and professional. Top to bottom: Cianci house, 1933. Hollyburn cabin, 1920s. Rush House, 1923. Opposite page: Creek/Van Damm house, 1962.

All photos by John Moir

West Coast Modern architecture is a legacy of the decades when imaginative designers created buildings that merged with the coastal landscape.

Top: Smith house II, ca. 1968. Architects: Erickson and Massey. *Photo by John Fulker, West Van Museum Collection 1.1.113.027*

Right: Catton house, ca. 1968. Architects: Erickson and Massey. *Photo by John Moir*

Below: B.C. Binning House, ca. 1941. Designer: B.C. Binning. *Photo by John Moir*

Above: Downs house, 1979. Architect: Barry Downs. *Drawing courtesy of the architect*

Below: Neoteric house, 1950. Architect: Fred Hollingsworth. *Photo by Mike Bernard*

Top: Duke house, 1954. Designer: Lewis Construction Company.
Photo by John Moir

Right: Griblin house, 1972. Architect: Barry Griblin.
Photo by John Moir

Below: Beaton House, 1965. Architect: Arthur Mudry.
Photo by John Moir

Top: Taylor house, 1983. Architect: Daniel Evan White.
Photo by John Moir

Left: Simons house, 1970. Architects: Erickson and Massey; Bruno Freschi, project designer.
Photo by Selwyn Pullan

Top: Safeguarding heritage—the Rush house (page x) will be preserved by adding two new buildings to the lot. *Illustration courtesy Michael Geller*

Below: Looking to the future—increasing density while preserving the landscape will be a challenge in West Van in the years to come. *Illustration courtesy Grosvenor Americas*

Perched on solid rock, the McNab house of 1956 exudes a restrained modernist confidence. Duncan McNab designed a group of graceful post-and-beam family homes along Westmount Road. *West Vancouver Museum Collection, Gift of Selwyn Pullan. S. Pullan photo*

itself, with designs creating outdoor "rooms" where gardens and natural forms extended the design of the house. Architect Duncan McNab built his 1956 home with a tree enframed in its entrance, so that it could grow through the roof. The living and sleeping quarters fitted above and around a rocky outcrop.

Barry Downs was one of the leading architects in "melding architecture with landscape." The Rayer residence, which he designed while in a brief working relationship with Fred Hollingsworth in 1963, combined "existing trees and shrubbery . . . with a restrained list of native species." Here "nature reigns supreme, providing an ever-delightful and evolving experience."[72] His own home, built in 1979 on a rocky precipice overlooking the Strait of Georgia, expresses "an ever-changing ecosystem [that] adds to the sensory experience of the house."[73]

Arthur Erickson designed artist Gordon Smith's second house, a remarkable multi-level 1,700-square-foot structure, costing $34,000, in 1965. This airy house, which gives the feeling of being in nature even when indoors, is one of five buildings given the Prix du XXe siècle for "nationally significant architecture," featuring clean, simple lines and lots of wood and glass. Erickson commented, "I wanted the Smith house to reveal the site in the same way that I had found it revealed to me when I first walked into it[74]....Descending square pavilions surround the central courtyard containing a reflecting pool and decks that bridge the different levels."[75] Erickson's partnership with long-term West Vancouver

Massive fir and cedar beams allowed for large expanses of glass in the ground-breaking Porter house of 1948. Landscaping was largely left to Mother Nature in this creekside house, whose interior seems perfectly at home with its exterior.
West Vancouver Museum Collection, Gift of John Fulker. John Fulker photo

resident Geoffrey Massey between 1963 and 1972 also resulted in many innovative homes.

Perhaps there is a connection between architectural styles and how the notion of family and the role of women were being reconfigured in the post-war years. In West Vancouver, architect John Porter's house (1948–49) kept housework to a minimum. Floors, walls and ceilings required little or no maintenance, and glass areas could be cleaned with a big squeegee mop. He received the 1952 Massey award for best house in Canada.

Extended families, if they existed, were now often widely dispersed, placing a greater onus on the nuclear family. For the first time, parents raised their children isolated from the support of older relatives, and needed the unobstructed space a modernist home provides, which enabled them to easily monitor their children's activities. Now, as the family undergoes another reconfiguration with fewer children, perhaps other architectural forms are called for.

Whereas architects designed most of the innovative houses, builders ensured the quality of the end product. In 1956, Alex Browning organized the Parade of Homes along Bonnymuir Drive where competing builders demonstrated modern innovations in show homes. Contractors Eric and Mel Lauder, who both designed their own homes and worked with architects, owned one of the largest building companies. *Western Living Magazine* credits master builders like the Lauders with allowing architects the opportunity to take chances. "In many projects . . . the builder becomes a sounding board and suggestion box for the architect." The result of quality construction "exists in stairs that don't creak, walls that are mathematically plumb and in tiny, unseen details that offer a perfection that can only be sensed."[76] The Lauder brothers built over three hundred homes in the Lower Mainland, with nearly a hundred in West Vancouver.

Later Iterations

Modernism was a magnificent experiment, but it had a short life. The young architects had burst onto the scene after the Second World War with the optimistic belief that modernism should promote a more egalitarian society, with architecture, in Berwick's words, "a people's profession." This did not happen, at least in West Vancouver, where a combination of forces, especially the price of land, pointed architects to design houses that only the more affluent could afford. Many of the clients who could afford a private architect opted for more conservative structures.

Along with the need for openness that characterized modernist homes, humans also need separate spaces. Perhaps when many people are confronted with chaotic developments in the modern world, they feel an even deeper need for the darkness and security of a cave (or perhaps a castle) than for openness. Some consider many of the houses built in the 1970s and '80s by private developers aesthetic disasters, but they responded to real human needs.

Modernism went on the back burner for a number of years, but more recently modernist traditions have asserted themselves in a number of larger projects. Some incorporate much of the same aesthetic, adding a greater environmental sense that technological advances and building-code changes have made possible. As a recent BPP brochure expresses, "In our furthest area of Rodgers, our vision is to create Contemporary West Coast architecture, following the magnificent style of Seattle-based architect James Cutler, and Jim Olson, known for designing a Bill Gates residence."

The Gleneagles Community Centre by Patkau Architects is perhaps the best example in West Vancouver of an institutional building adapting modernism to a contemporary context. Designed by John and Patricia Patkau, massive Douglas fir beams and openness to light impart a spirit of community space. It is heated and cooled through a low-intensity radiant temperature system—no heating vents or radiators. In architect Barry Downs's words, it is "attuned to the mountains behind, the protective shell mitigates a drop in grade level and inventively accommodates both high and low level ceiling activity areas." Former West Vancouver mayor Mark Sager regrets that original plans to locate it on the east side of the road were changed so that it could be located on the west side of the road next to the golf course—at an extra cost of $6 million to reroute the road. But it is still a wonderful community space, providing a rendezvous for those in the western communities.

A number of current firms build on the legacy of modernism. Battersby Howat has worked extensively in the Lower Mainland, bringing to their work "a fully integrated, holistic approach to design." They have built a number of homes in West Vancouver, including a recent residence on Fairmile Road. One of their best-known projects has been the renovation of the Helmut and Hildegard Eppich house, a post-and-beam home designed by Erickson in 1972, with Cornelia Oberlander as landscape architect. Built into a steep incline in long lateral bands, it was impressive architecturally, but unfortunately prone to leaks; wood construction on the wet West Coast has a limited life span. In 2015, Battersby Howat undertook a major renovation that addressed this problem and incorporated a greater practicality in the construction. As David Battersby said, "The house may leak, but the architecture is bigger than the leak."

Splyce Design, with architect Nigel Parish, is one of the newer firms carrying on the tradition of modernism, exploring "how thoughtfully designed objects and spaces have the ability to inspire, engage our senses, and ultimately influence our quality of life." In West Vancouver, their Russet residence, built into a steep slope, nestles "itself into the hill while also projecting out over it to maximize views and connectivity to the landscape." To avoid compromising the fragile environment, portions of the main and upper floor are cantilevered back past the foundation to allow the native vegetation to grow up as a wild forest floor.

From the early ski cabins a century past to the more recent modernist homes, the best of West Vancouver's architecture has expressed a creative individuality combined with a harmonious incorporation of the natural world, while technological developments have enhanced compatibility with the environment. Its rugged but breathtakingly beautiful landscape has provided a unique setting that has inspired architects and builders, and continues to do so.

"It's [Canada's] a garden of many different flowers."

—West Vancouver resident Farid Rohani

Young fire jumpers celebrate Norooz in 2017.

Photo by Cindy Goodman, NSNews

07

SHAPING THE FUTURE

TENTATIVE DANCES WITH DIVERSITY

Urbanist Richard Florida has explained how communities with a high quality of life attract new residents with diverse lifestyles and ethnicities. The resulting inclusion increases the human wealth on which a community can draw. Although West Vancouver's economic diversity is limited, its ethnic diversity is increasing. Iranians and Chinese presently make up the largest non-European ethnic groups in West Vancouver, slowly modifying West Vancouver's Caucasian core. In the 2016 census, 6,185 (14.6 per cent) of residents spoke Mandarin or Cantonese as a first language and 3,785 (8.9 per cent) gave Persian as their first language. Over 1,600 West Vancouverites did not speak English at this time. The proportion of immigrants in West Vancouver (people born outside of Canada) increased to 41 per cent in 2011 compared with 40 per cent in Metro Vancouver, although many of these have lived here for generations.

Iranians have immigrated to Canada in successive waves over the past half century. Although a few arrived earlier, their community in West Vancouver generally started forming as a result of the 1979 Islamic revolution. Many Baha'i also left Iran, as the new Islamist government considered them apostates and subjected them to persecution. Others came from the US after the Iranian hostage situation in 1979–81 made

The controversial Edgewater building, with its imposing symmetry, dominates the landscape at the 23rd Street waterfront. A crane in the background suggests that it is soon to be joined, and possibly eclipsed, by what may be yet another contentious structure. *Photo by John Moir*

them (for a time) less welcome in that country, and more escaped from the devastating effects of the Iran–Iraq war, which ended in 1988. A later group, which has generally made its money in Iran, has arrived within the last decade, although the meteoric rise of house prices in West Vancouver may be slowing their influx. Some say the Canadian community was not so welcoming in the early days, but now there seem to be few problems with integrating into the Canadian mosaic.

A number have been active in local politics and others have been successful in high tech and real estate. Order of Canada appointee Hassan Khosrowshahi came to Vancouver in 1981 and founded the major electronics company Future Shop; in 2012 he had a net worth of $940 million. Shahran Malekyazdi made his mark in real estate, establishing the Millennium Corporation with his brother Peter. His West Vancouver projects include Edgewater, a luxurious apartment building at 2288 Bellevue, designed by New York architect Robert Stern, with fifteen floors at one suite per floor. This was built on the site of an earlier Edgewater apartment, a three-storey, twenty-unit complex built in 1953.

Although the later Edgewater was judged Canada's best multi-family development in 2006, not all joined the chorus. Architectural writer Robin Ward took vigorous exception to what he considered its insensitive disjunction with local architecture, scorning it as a "15-storey monster house…like a guest in a toga who has turned up to the wrong fancy dress ball." No doubt a side effect of becoming a more international community means that respect for local architectural traditions may not be as strong. Other Millennium efforts have received a more positive reception. Although their Evelyn Drive apartment project proved financially disastrous (see pp. 86–87), Onni largely took over Millennium's design, which has generally gained acceptance.

Art can be an important cultural ambassador. Iran has a rich tradition of poetry and the visual arts, and many accomplished Iranian artists make West Vancouver their home for all or part of the year. Houshang Seyhoun (1920–2014), an architect and visual artist who served as dean of arts at the School of Fine Arts and Architecture at the University of Tehran, left Iran at the time of the revolution. As an architect, he designed Tehran's central railway station and a building of the Iranian Natural Congress. His intricate, complex images based on scenes from nature have been exhibited throughout the world including, in 1984, at the West Vancouver Memorial Library. One of his intricate pen-and-ink drawings

With Persian residents come Persian markets and unique products, adding to the cultural mix of the community. *Photo by John Moir*

is featured in *From Cottages to Community,* the centennial history of West Vancouver.

Parviz Tanavoli, who now divides his time between West Vancouver and Iran, is Iran's most renowned living artist. He has mounted solo exhibitions in Austria, Italy, Germany, the United States and Britain. Rather than follow Western traditions, he has created his own vision, infused with his deep knowledge of Iran's rich visual craft and literary heritage. He is especially known for his *heeches*, three-dimensional representations of the Persian word for "nothing." A 2015 film, *Parviz Tanavoli: Poetry in Bronze*, directed by Terence Turner, documents his journey of creation across three continents.

Many Iranians have built or bought huge houses, especially in the British Properties. BCIT professor Dr. Mory Ghomshei states that

Iranians are practical and build to an international rather than national style, although they do indeed like their houses big. Typically, a large house will have a space for guests and entertainment, and a smaller private section for the family. At get-togethers in the large room, the reading of traditional Persian poetry, often with musical accompaniment by a sitar or tar, both stringed instruments, provides an important cultural unifier.

The first Norooz, the Iranian festival celebrating the spring equinox, the birth of a new year and personal renewal, took place at Sentinel Secondary School in 1990. In this festival, people leap over fires to purify their spirits for the coming year. The Fire Festival and Norooz are now celebrated each spring at Ambleside Park where, as local resident Homa Mojiri says, "If you go and watch the sunset in Ambleside, that is really life."

The Chinese have a much longer history in the Lower Mainland. The early exclusions in the BPP were aimed largely at them, and for fifty years before that they were often victims of "whites-only" hiring policies. The emerging success of many ethnic Chinese following the Second World War has been complemented by many recent arrivals who have benefitted from China's resurgence. Some have brought great wealth to Canada, with many finding West Vancouver, and particularly the mansions of the British Properties, a congenial fit. Perhaps, like the early developers of BPP, their families are attracted by a safe and secure country in which to invest their money. Many newcomers retain businesses in China, with the man of the family often going back and forth between Canada and China to maintain his business. As many have said, Canada is a great place to raise a family but not so great for business—at least, not for them.

Developers and realtors have been quick to take advantage, targeting the Asian market in many ways. Feng shui, the Chinese art of positioning objects or structures so as to harmonize with spiritual forces, is an important factor informing the decisions of many Asians in buying a particular residence. The principle of harmony with the environment has found fertile soil in the Lower Mainland. Even those who may not believe in feng shui may renovate their houses according to its principles to make them more saleable to an Asian market. And West Vancouver's setting, with its sea views and proximity to hills and forests, much like Hong Kong, provides good energy.

Similarly, auspicious numbers attract some Asian buyers, with many realtors catering to that interest. The details of the desirability of different numbers are complicated, but basically eight is good (as the sound in

Cantonese is similar to an expression meaning "to make a fortune") while four is bad (as its sound is similar to the word for "death"). A recent check of listed prices for West Vancouver homes shows that 70–75 per cent contain at least one number eight. Fewer than 10 per cent contain the number four.

Despite the growing presence of Asian people in West Vancouver, or perhaps because of it, an edge of xenophobia persists, sometimes expressing itself in an unease at the number of people of visible minorities in a city that has been European for so long. There's no doubt that the nature of the community is changing in far deeper and subtler ways than the price of housing. But these are opportunities for unique fusions. The interplay between Canadian and Asian cultures can enrich and diversify our culture and economy. Western bluegrass and Chinese folk music reverberating against each other on the same stage creates something much more than the sum of their parts. An evening of Chinese folk dancing followed by a Western ballet provides new insights into both. Such interplay between Asian and Western cultures can build a unique community from the creative synergy of the two, just as Western culture is bringing profound social and cultural change to China and other Asian countries.

When the End of the Rainbow Is Not Enough

> We change the world one room at a time.
>
> —Peter Block, *Community: The Structure of Belonging*

West Vancouver is not only about big houses and big money. Although it has no homeless shelters, the North Shore Housing Centre in North Vancouver, with twenty-five transitional housing units, forty-five shelter beds and twenty extreme-weather sleeping mats, also accommodates some West Vancouver residents. North Shore Projects provides for clothing exchange and home visits. In 2017 the official homeless count found one hundred homeless on the North Shore, although local social service agencies estimate it could be much higher, perhaps as many as a thousand. The Hollyburn Family Services Society's Seniors at Risk Program supported forty-six seniors who were homeless or at risk of being homeless, and saved seventy West Vancouver seniors from eviction. Other older people may be living in multimillion-dollar homes, but still be cash poor. Homeless set up their tents from time to time in parks at Horseshoe Bay.

These physical problems are compounded by less tangible issues. As early as 1980, a report on the implications of limiting growth, by a committee chaired by former councillor and community activist Rod Day, warned that West Vancouver "may become socially isolated as the result of the wealth of its inhabitants, and it may become psychologically isolated as a result of the absence of children and young families." His concerns have been increasingly borne out in recent years, exacerbated by the influx of immigrants whose wealth often insulates them from the community support that could ease their integration into the mainstream of West Vancouver life.

The West Vancouver Community Foundation's 2016 Vital Signs reports a high rate of vulnerability among children in the British Properties, noting that 33 per cent of kindergartners may by unprepared for school linguistically, socially, physically, emotionally and in terms of general knowledge and skills. This relates "to the high proportion of immigrants settling in the area who are not accessing family support and educational services."

Working in partnership with UBC researchers who have been tracking childhood development across the province over several years, Sandra-Lynn Shortall, the district principal of Early Learning at West Vancouver Schools, realized that important community support was less accessible in some areas, especially for many new families residing in the British Properties. In 2014 she initiated the British Properties Family Hub, based at Chartwell Elementary School, with local partners. Housed in a portable on site, the program offers intergenerational activities and opportunities at low or no cost to facilitate stronger community connections.

For many families in the properties, the low housing density makes it difficult for children and their parents to interact with their neighbours. Nancy Farran, chair of the Community Foundation, suggests that the isolation of many residents in their luxurious homes discourages youngsters from socializing, deepening the linguistic divide. There's still no community park in the properties. In many families, one parent (most often the husband) works elsewhere or does business globally, while the remaining family members reside in Canada. The resulting isolation increases the time it takes to build relationships and understand the importance of social interaction for healthy social-emotional development.

Establishing intercultural bridges challenges both those providing and receiving services. Many may bring from their home countries a mistrust of the government and apprehension of any initiatives perceived as government mandated. Many have left lives of success and power for a Canadian life where their previous qualifications and experience are unrecognized. Letting go of the past to build a new future is not easy. Once made aware of opportunities, Shortall finds that most families welcome ways to connect with neighbours and friends in a diverse environment, learning new skills and making valuable contributions to their community. The children naturally adapt to their new lives the quickest.

Numerous programs offered through the Hub have taken a creative approach to ameliorating this alienation. A Mandarin dance group composed of women with school-age children has been highly successful. "Before Bedtime Adventures" has linked grandfathers, fathers and children in such activities as building birdhouses and going on nature walks. A Mandarin book club has also been popular. IPALS (Immigrant Parents as Literacy Supporters), offered in Farsi and Mandarin, enables preschool children and their parents to develop language and literacy skills to adapt to their community and prepare them for school. StrongStart also develops social/emotional and language/literacy skills in preschoolers.

Shortall and community partners invited volunteers to take part in planning a Canada 150 celebration at nearby Sentinel Seconday School. Volunteers from the properties and the rest of West Vancouver participated enthusiastically, producing and coordinating a street party in late September 2017 that attracted about six hundred people. The community is evolving and coming together in new and creative ways, with those at the Family Hub taking on ever more active roles in community building.

Many West Vancouverites, particularly recent arrivals, also participate in the North Shore Multicultural Centre's programs, which work to bridge cultural gaps between Canada and their country of origin. What does community mean? What does friendship across cultures look like? In facilitated conversations, new arrivals interact with people from the mainstream community, including Indigenous people. Meharoona Ghomi, manager of Community Connections at the multicultural centre, sees these meetings as a two-way process in which those outside the culture learn the skills needed for integration, while those from within the culture modify their perceptions to accommodate new realities. Each grain of salt (or perhaps red pepper?) changes the flavour of the stew.

Many of these meetings take place at the West Vancouver Library, which also holds story times in Farsi, Korean and Russian. Quite often the actual activity is secondary to the way group activity facilitates communication. Language classes and numerous other programs help newcomers in the difficult journey to belonging.

Former British Properties manager Jim McLean argues that "the future belongs to the future"—that is, too often planning is left in the hands of people who will not be around to experience the results. But what kind of city will the young people want to enjoy? Like Ebenezer Howard more than a century ago, he argues for the advantages of having central control of large parcels of land to prevent developmental fragmentation. False Creek has benefited in this way, he says, from having Li Ka-Shing at the helm. And BPP's extensive holdings give it a unique power. McLean has no final answers, but expresses frustration that West Vancouver is not dealing with the big issues. Planning, he argues, needs a person of strength and vision who can act as an intermediary between the developer and the public, bringing the two together for concerted action. Some, including former mayor Mark Sager and current mayor Michael Smith, find much in these views to recommend them. Perhaps it's time for another Roy Pidgeon, whose actions in the 1940s directly prevented West Vancouver from succumbing to commercial sprawl.

At a recent series of workshops in West Vancouver organized by the West Vancouver Community Foundation, community representatives wrestled with how to reconfigure the community to ensure that those from elsewhere and those already here can find their place in the sun. A sense of urgency pervaded the discussion, a feeling that, without action, West Vancouver will become a Beverly Hills North, where a small number of rich live in splendid isolation, dependent on a large service class that lives elsewhere. To go back to Steve Jobs, "Design is not so much how it looks, as how it works." West Vancouver needs to work for all its citizens, including those who will move here in the future. Even though the community infrastructure of the library, community centres and parks are models of the latest achievements in design, gaining everyone's participation is a slow and arduous process.

The conversations that can lead to community renewal need to

Members of the local Indigenous community representing the Squamish, Tsleil-Waututh and Musqueam First Nations perform a traditional welcome blessing on the site of their ancestral land in Ambleside at the opening ceremony of the Harmony Arts Festival, 2018. *Photo by John Moir*

include all or at least a cross-section of all members of the community. It concerned many that few if any Squamish from the Capilano Reserve attended any of the workshops. And the super affluent, whether recent arrivals or longer-term residents, seemed at best under represented. The conditions must be fostered that will make people want to belong, to realize how important it is for community health—and their health. Perhaps long-time Indigenous advocate Maisie Hurley is right when she says Indigenous people "don't want to assimilate. They are wonderful people with magnificent traditions of their own."[77]

The legacy of community commitment that runs from Francis Caulfeild through Joseph Leyland and Roy Pidgeon and a host of mostly unsung heroes is one of a belief that West Vancouver is a special place with a precious birthright. Their past dedication has created a unique place that embodies much of the best of human endeavour, but all must now join the party. Barbara McMillan, the lead researcher and writer for the Vital Signs reports, argues that a sense of belonging is fundamental to individual and community health. We must create conditions for people to connect. The health of everyone in the community, and therefore of the community itself, depends on the success of this dialogue.

From beachfront cottages to palatial homes, the history of West Vancouver shows that it has been anything but static, and it's a safe bet that the future will not be like the present. In 2010, then mayor Pamela Goldsmith-Jones said, "To keep what we have, we'll have to change." Through community discussions a vision that fuses the future with the people who will then call it home can be made concrete.

> People buy homes like stepping stones, and West Vancouver is the last stop.
>
> —Realtor Mark Angell

The Bellevue by Cressey will send luxury skyward in West Van.

Photo courtesy Cressey Development Group

08

HOW HIGH IS UP?

While it's true that everything now costs more than it used to, house prices in West Vancouver have risen even faster than the price of an ice cream cone, and some of us remember the good old days when a cone was a nickel. Occasionally the rise slows, and even contracts slightly, but then the prices surge with alarming speed, inducing panic in prospective buyers. Some houses sell for more than a thousand times what they did in the 1930s.

A combination of global forces and local circumstances has driven this rise in the Lower Mainland. A network of high rollers has exploited Canada's easygoing open-for-business policy by manipulating or openly flouting Canadian financial regulations, buying and selling houses like stocks, especially in the Lower Mainland. And West Vancouver's attractiveness makes it a prime target. Its mountainous geography and extensive waterfront constricts the places where houses can be built, squeezing the supply and placing a unique upward pressure on prices.

According to a study by Demographia, Vancouver ranks third in world house prices, after Hong Kong and Sydney, Australia; West Vancouver is at or near the top of house prices in the Vancouver area. This measure of affordability compares the median price of a home with the median income: in 2017 Vancouver house prices were 12.6 times the median household income. But this study doesn't take into account the fact that the size of homes in Hong Kong and some other places is generally much smaller than those in Vancouver; tiny apartments of 200 square feet are culturally accepted in Hong Kong in a way they would not be in Vancouver, particularly West Vancouver. Toronto-based Condo.ca argues that a more accurate comparison is through the price per square foot. In their comparison of eighteen cities, Hong Kong is still number one, with

The innovative architects of the mid-century worked with the natural landscape in West Van. More recently, developers often treat landscape as profit potential, excavating into every square foot of it to reshape it into maximum living space.
Photo by John Moir

property costing $3,086 per square foot. Vancouver is down at number eight at $900 a square foot, although a lot of new places are coming on the market at $2,000 a square foot or higher.

But does that mean Vancouver (and West Vancouver) is relatively affordable after all? Only theoretically. Demand and supply are only two of the important parameters. The demand—based on West Vancouver's enviable beauty, diverse outdoor activities, stable political environment and opportunities for stimulating work—is undeniably high and generally beyond the control of the municipality (not that it would want such control). The supply of housing can be increased, but the supply of land, the main factor in a house's cost, is fixed. With the price of land remaining at 80 to 90 per cent of the total price, increasing the housing supply will not have a significant effect on prices as long as the size of residences remains at or near their current level. In the central area of Ambleside and Dundarave, most houses are assessed in the $100,000 to $200,000 range, with the land valued at upwards of ten times that. Farther out, in the pricier subdivisions where the houses are generally newer and bigger, the discrepancy between land and house prices is not so dramatic. Some of the houses are valued at over a million, but the land is generally more than four million.

In July 2017 the price of a detached home in West Vancouver averaged $3.1 million, while an apartment averaged $1.1 million. Phase 2 of the municipal OCP review stated that, on average, a family would need an annual income of $500,000 to purchase a single-family home, and $180,000 (twice the West Vancouver median household income[78]) to buy an apartment. With few exceptions, salaried people without other substantial financial resources can no longer buy houses or even apartments. The price of housing, driven by wealth rather than income, is disconnected from local wealth-building, and the increased mobility of the wealthy drives house prices ever higher. In 2016, 9 per cent of houses in West Vancouver sat unoccupied, further inflating housing prices. Many may have been purchased for investment and may be inhabited for only part of the year, or not at all.

In West Vancouver high prices have distorted local demographics. The proportion of the elderly, who may have purchased houses in more affordable times, has increased. At the same time, in 2016, 3,950 West Vancouver residents were aged twenty-five to thirty-nine, a 45 per cent drop since 1996. This is no doubt largely attributable to affordability, but perhaps also to many younger people wanting a more stimulating lifestyle than the peaceful serenity West Vancouver currently offers.

There is a huge difference between the average West Vancouver home and the much larger homes of recent years. That average $3.1 million bungalow in West Vancouver is no larger than bungalows elsewhere, and might sell for a twentieth of that price in Kapuskasing. But for an additional few hundred thousand, a property owner can build a house three times the size in West Vancouver and sell it for five million or more, which makes knocking down a house and rebuilding financially attractive. Houses often fall victim to the wrecking ball long before their usefulness has expired.

High housing costs have made it increasingly difficult for employers to attract workers. Recently, of 144 police officers, only twelve lived in West Vancouver. How would that affect response time in a major earthquake? (Apparently a barge for transportation across the inlet is being considered as a contingency.) Fewer than 10 per cent of the municipal staff live in the city where they work. Without minimizing the problem, though, it should be pointed out that many of those who cannot afford West Vancouver live in slightly more affordable neighbouring North Vancouver. For example, while only 16 per cent of West Vancouver teachers live in West Vancouver, 63 per cent live on the North Shore. But as prices in North Vancouver also escalate, the boundaries of affordability move east up the Fraser Valley. Between 2001 and 2011, West Vancouver lost 1,700 jobs. It's more appealing to work where you live than commute for an hour or two each way. Many Vancouverites deeply resent being pushed to the margins of their community.

The extent to which offshore money has increased the prices of local housing is hard to define, but there is no doubt it has done so. In 2015 an estimated trillion dollars was moved out of China.[79] In that year Chinese buyers put an estimated $12 billion into Vancouver real estate, accounting for 33 per cent of the city's real estate sales.[80] This influx of Chinese money appears to be slowing, as there is now a limit of $50,000 on the money an individual can take out of China, and new regulations in Canada are causing some investors to look for other markets. But it certainly has not stopped. Crowdfunding has been used recently as a way of buying real estate, with clients in China putting up cash to purchase houses in return for a high rate of return. West Vancouver councillor Mary-Ann Booth has noted that at open houses for the most expensive properties, up to four out of five potential buyers typically speak Mandarin or Farsi, with some buying two or three houses. Many long-term residents are no doubt surprised but pleased to see their homes escalate enormously in value.

The Globe and Mail's Kathy Tomlinson[81] has partially penetrated the shadowy world of house flipping and international financial manipulation and found that speculators often hold properties just long enough for them to rise significantly in value. Absentee foreign clients bankroll everything, often bypassing banks, with lenders getting generous returns of up to 15 per cent annually from the profits. The Canadian government is in this way deprived of substantial tax revenue. A Chinese-Canadian accountant estimates he has filed returns for a thousand clients in similar circumstances. "Another Vancouver accountant told *The Globe* that she and her colleagues see questionable real estate transactions all the time, which they believe have contributed to skyrocketing prices." While offshore money factors heavily in the escalation of prices, local developers and realtors have been anything but reluctant in capitalizing on the millions to be made by flipping properties.

There's a haunting fear in some that the main economic driver of the Lower Mainland and its escalating prices is its enormously attractive location, but what does it actually produce? How long can a gorgeous location continue to drive the economy?

There's plenty of blame to go around. Xenophobia is tempting, but the escalation of housing prices is the product of forces of greed that know no national boundaries. Local governments can get addicted to the enormous amount of money flowing in for development projects, whether it's from Canada or elsewhere. Although the millions of dollars developers pay West Vancouver's municipal government in return for relaxing zoning restrictions is intended largely as a fund for affordable housing, the high price of land limits these possibilities.

It's hard to ignore the cultural echoes between West Vancouver and such past developments as the foreign precincts in Shanghai, where foreigners lived in palatial residences and worked on the Bund in European-styled offices, becoming wealthy off the backs of local labourers who commuted from the outlying low-rent districts. So does this mean West Vancouver is becoming a colony where the wealthy who have made West Vancouver their home rely on service providers from elsewhere? Or an overpriced cottage country?

Moderately priced rental units are rare in West Van. Those seeking affordable rents must increasingly look elsewhere. *Photo by John Moir*

More rentals might help affordability, but current rents are high and apartments scarce. The vacancy rate in 2018 is 0.2 per cent, and only ninety-one rental units have been added or approved in the past forty years. Four units built at Dundarave Landing were designated rentals for a ten-year period that expired in 2017. Sixteen units were added at the Water's Edge apartments. More recent additions include thirty units in the Onni development in the last apartment building next to Taylor Way. At Hollyburn Gardens, 21st and Bellevue, council has recently approved the construction of forty-one rental apartments. More are possible in developments on the eastern edge of West Vancouver. The average rental for a one-bedroom apartment in West Vancouver, $2,600 in October 2017 according to PadMapper, is the highest in BC. It's not likely this will decrease substantially anytime soon.

In 2018, current mayor Michael Smith yearns for affordable accommodation for the younger people—those who have young families and would actively contribute to community life. He notes a disjunction between housing and the population's needs, with the community having more than twice as many bedrooms as in the '70s, but fewer than half the

Once a relatively self-contained community of quiet neighbourhoods, West Van has evolved into a worldly and active living space for affluent residents. *Photo by John Moir*

number of children. Large numbers of parents from North Vancouver and other communities as well as many from overseas are attracted by the excellent educational facilities in West Vancouver. Meanwhile, many schools have been struggling to find suitable teachers.

West Vancouver has all the attributes a community could wish: natural beauty, wealth and an educated and cultured population in a stable political environment. This is immense capital on which to build. The conversations that will enable West Vancouver to open up, to transform into a place with a greater diversity of age and income will be long and difficult. Those conversations are not only necessary but need to include a broad cross-section of local residents in them, from the Squamish people, who are the original inhabitants of the area, to the newest arrivals, who are bringing fresh perspectives to the community. The conversations themselves are an important part of the solution to any and every problem, as they bring with them a breaking down of artificial walls. Francis Caulfeild, Joseph Leyland and other builders

Older buildings in the Ambleside commercial/rental area are showing their age, and are being eclipsed by new luxury apartments such as the Grosvenor development, its first phase completed in 2018. *Photo by John Moir*

of West Vancouver have left a rich legacy of dedicated community commitment. Fortunately the current community has an extraordinary number of intelligent, committed people who can build on this legacy. The next few years will require their creativity and innovation to do so.

ACKNOWLEDGEMENTS

A number of people read all or part of the manuscript, providing me with advice and helpful corrections. These include Geoff Croll, Kiriki Watanabe, Rick Amantea, Dorothy Moore, Barry Downs, Reto Tschan and Rod Day.

Reto Tschan, West Vancouver archivist, and the staff of the West Vancouver Memorial Library (especially Julie Backer) have been indispensable keys to providing materials crucial to the writing of this book, going many extra kilometres.

David Hawkins, Rod Day, Steve Nicholls and Jim Bailey helped familiarize me with the municipality's ongoing role in shaping their community; other municipal staff were helpful in providing me with important documents. Former mayor Mark Sager provided me with many intriguing perspectives, while current mayor Michael Smith and councillor Nora Gambioli provided a contemporary view.

Lib and Chris Wooten, Dianne Sherwood and Angus Stuart educated me on the rich history and current debates that have defined and are defining Lower Caulfeild.

Crowds gather at Dundarave on July 1st to watch fireworks. *Photo by John Moir*

Rick Amantea provided much helpful information on Park Royal, present and future. The research of UBC students Maia Janz and Coris Nickerson on Park Royal and British Pacific Properties, respectively, was useful.

Geoff Croll and Jim McLean, current and former managers of British Pacific Properties, gave generously of their time and knowledge.

Delaina Bell put me in touch with Barbara McMillan, chief writer of the Vital Signs reports, who introduced me to important but less publicized aspects of West Vancouver. Sandra-Lynn Shortall and Beverly Pausche of the British Properties Hub deepened my understanding of West Vancouver's more recent arrivals and their influence, as did Meharoona Ghomi and Shabnam Rohbani of the North Shore Multicultural Centre. Shiva Kashi, Dr. Mory Ghomshei and Ramin Mahjoori shared freely their first-hand knowledge of the Iranian community and its many contributions to West Vancouver.

Modernist architect Ned Pratt's son Peter provided insightful stories and information about his father and modernist architecture. Michael Barnes, Barry Downs and James Bligh also added to my information and provided me with good leads. Thanks to Erick Villagomez for his information on urban planning and the groundbreaking publication, *Shaping Spaces,* for which he writes.

Thanks to long-time surveyor Bill Chapman for providing generous access to his knowledge.

FINANCIAL SUPPORTERS OF DREAMERS AND DESIGNERS

The West Vancouver Historical Society sincerely thanks the following, who have generously supported the publication of *Dreamers and Designers: The Shaping of West Vancouver*.

Members of the Leyland Family

Ed and Jill Berwick and family
Michael and Barbara Evans
Anton and Anne Evans Kramer
Dorothy and Keith Moore and Mary E. Moore
Susan Rhodes

Corporate and Charitable Organizations

British Pacific Properties
District of West Vancouver
Michael Geller and Associates
West Vancouver Community Foundation
West Vancouver Memorial Library

Individuals

Jean and Chris Adshead
Julie Backer
David Barker
Michael Barnes
Eric Bendrot
Mary-Ann Booth
Anne and Court Brousson
Jim Carter
Joan Cox
Rod Day
Susan Dirassar
Margaret Etchell
Don and Donna Fletcher
Pamela Friedrick

Jacqueline Gijssen
Peter Hall
Raydelle Hyde
Margaret Jaffary
Jeanette Keller
Bob and Kathie Lefeaux
Roddy MacKenzie
Nonie and Glenn McCuaig
Susan Webb Parkes
Margaret and Tom Taylor
Wendy and Lorne Topham
Fred Van Aggelen
Joyce Wehnan
Georgie Wilson
David Woodhouse

West Van's dominant demographic is long past skateboarding, but they can always watch from the Seawalk at Ambleside. *Photo by John Moir*

WEST VANCOUVER HISTORICAL SOCIETY'S BOOK COMMITTEE

The book committee has produced three books over the years celebrating and preserving various aspects of West Vancouver's history. The first book was *Cottages to Community: The Story of West Vancouver's Neighbourhoods*, the second was *Arrivals and Departures: The Ferries and People of Horseshoe Bay* and the third one is *Dreamers and Designers: The Shaping of West Vancouver*.

Basically the same people have been responsible for all three books. The book committee has been chaired by Jim Carter; Francis Mansbridge was the author, John Moir was the photo archivist, Colleen Wood was the designer for the first two books and Michael Barnes and David Barker have been representatives of the Historical Society Board.

At the top of 26th Street, high above Burrard Inlet, a jogger makes his way across the pedestrian overpass. *Photo by John Moir*

SELECTED SOURCES

Apart from personal contacts, the West Vancouver Archives and the West Vancouver Memorial Library have been my main sources for the numerous details that weave the fabric of a developing community. Other sources are indicated here.

Thanks to the Leyland family, especially Dorothy Leyland, whose extensive family papers helped fill in some of the history and activities that made Joe Leyland one of the key figures in the shaping of West Vancouver.

Art Gallery of Greater Vancouver. *B.C. Binning: A Classical Spirit*, 1986.

Baker, Simon, with Verna Kirkness. *Khot-la-Cha, The Autobiography of Simon Baker*. Vancouver: Douglas & McIntyre, 1994.

Bellerby, Greg, et al. *Living Spaces: The Architecture of Fred Thornton Hollingsworth*. Vancouver: Blueimprint, ca. 2005.

———, ed. *The West Coast Modern House: Vancouver Residential Architecture*. Vancouver: Figure 1/Charles H. Scott Gallery, 2014.

Berelowitz, Lance. *Dream City: Vancouver and the Global Imagination*. Vancouver: Douglas & McIntyre, 2005.

Berger, Heinz. *An Adventure on Two Continents*. West Vancouver, 2015.

"A Bit of England in West Vancouver." *Vancouver Sun Magazine Section*, August 22, 1936, pp. 1–2.

Block, Peter. *Community: The Structure of Belonging*. San Francisco: Berrett-Koehler Pubishers, Inc., 2008.

British Pacific Properties. "Envisioning Notebook." Presented by British Pacific Properties, April 2000.

Chancey, Jonathan. *The Story of Architecture*. New York: DK Publishing, 2000.

Croll, Geoff. "British Pacific Properties: Making History in West Vancouver for 85 Years." Presentation to West Vancouver Historical Society, March 15, 2017.

Day, Rod. "The Citizens' Planning Forum." Unpublished article.

_______. "Waterfront Acquisition in West Vancouver, Ambitious, Controversial and Forward Thinking." *BC History* 51.3 (fall 2018).

Downs, Barry. *Melding Architecture with Landscape*. West Vancouver Museum, 2013.

Dunlop, Herbert Francis. *Andy Paull: As I Knew Him and Understood His Times.* Vancouver: Order of the O.M.I. of St. Paul's Province, 1989.

Finch, Peter. "History of British Properties." Lecture given at the West Vancouver Historical Society, 1992.

Florida, Richard. *The Rise of the Creative Class.* New York: Basic Books, 2002.

———. *Who's Your City?* Toronto: Random House, 2008.

———. *The New Urban Crisis.* New York: Basic Books, 2017.

Froome, Gavin. *Coast Modern: Three Generations of Inspired Living. A Film Tracing the Roots of West Coast Modern.* DVD, 113 min.

Grosvenor. *Ambleside Development.* October 17, 2012.

"Homelessness on the North Shore." Report of the North Shore Task Force on Homelessness, September 2000.

Howard, Ebenezer. *Garden Cities of Tomorrow.* London: Faber and Faber, 1945. Originally published in 1898 as *Tomorrow: A Peaceful Path to Reform.*

Humphreys, Derrick, as told to John Munro. *The Making of a Grey Panther: The Derrick Humphreys Story.* Vancouver: Ronsdale, 2006.

Jacobs, Jane. *Dark Age Ahead.* Toronto: Random House, 2004.

———. *The Death and Life of Great American Cities.* Toronto: Random House, 1961.

Jamieson, Eric. *The Native Voice: The History of Canada's First Aboriginal Newspaper and Its Founder Maisie Hurley.* Halfmoon Bay, BC: Caitlin Press, 2016.

Johanson, Roff, "Democracy and Municipal Government in West Vancouver: The Case of 320 Taylor Way." *BC Studies* 91–92 (Autumn and Winter 1991–92), pp. 152–172.

Johnston, Kay. *The Amazing Mazie Baker, the Squamish Nation's Warrior Elder.* Halfmoon Bay, BC: Caitlin Press, 2016.

Kalman, Harold. *A History of Canadian Architecture*, Vol. 2. Toronto: Oxford University Press, 1994.

Khatsahlano, August Jack, and Dominic Charlie. *Squamish Legends.* Edited by Oliver N. Wells, Charles Chamberlain, and Frank T. Coan, 1966.

[Lauder, Sylvia]. *Lauder Bros., Custom Home Builders 1948–1997.* 2002.

Liscombe, R.W. *The New Spirit: Modern Architecture in Vancouver.* Montreal: Canadian Centre for Architecture, 1997.

Luxton, Don, and Lilia D'Acres. *Lions Gate Bridge.* Vancouver: Talon Books, 1999.

Mansbridge, Francis. *From Cottages to Community.* West Vancouver Historical Society, 2011.

———. *Hollyburn: The Mountain and the City*. Vancouver: Ronsdale Press, 2008.

Matthews, Major James. *Early Vancouver: Narratives of Pioneers of Vancouver, B.C.* Vol. II. Vancouver: Brock Webber Printing Co., 1932.

Montgomery, Charles. *Happy City: Transforming Our Lives Through Urban Design.* New York: Farrar, Strauss and Giroux, 2013.

Morningstar, Janet, and Robert Taylor. *Spuraway.* West Vancouver: 2012.

Mulally, Frederic. *The Silver Salver: The Story of the Guinness Family*. London: Granada Publishing, 1981.

Oberlander, Peter H., and Ira M. Robinson. "Living and Working in West Vancouver, British Columbia: An Economic Analysis as a Basis for Community Planning." Corporation of the Municipal District of West Vancouver, 1954.

O'Donnell, Brendan. "Indian and non-Native Use of the Capilano River: An Historical Perspective." Fisheries and Oceans, Canada, Policy and Program Planning, Native Affairs Division, Issue 5, n.d.

Patterson, Frederick. "A Financial History of the Corporation of the District of West Vancouver." M.A. thesis, UBC, 1928.

Payne, Ruth. *Portals of Our Past: A History of the Ferry Building Gallery 1913–1997*. West Vancouver, Cultural Services, 1997.

Pettit, Barbara, and Patricia Gallagher. *Standing Up for Nature. Eagleridge Bluffs: A Study of Protest and Disobedience.* West Vancouver: Red-Legged Frog Society, 2015.

Pratt, Ned. "Canadian Domestic Architecture in British Columbia." *Journal of the Royal Architectural Institute of Canada*, June 1947.

Ramsey, Bruce. *A Place of Excellence: A Chronicle of West Vancouver 1912–1987.* District of West Vancouver, 1986.

Rodgers Creek Area Plan. District of West Vancouver, 2008.

Rodgers Creek Owners' Association. *Rodgers Creek Neighbourhood Plan*. April 30, 2001.

Sartori Environmental Services. *Rodgers Creek Area 6—Phase 2 Development Permit Environmental Management Plan.* North Vancouver, August 2007.

Spears, James. "Cut Off by Broken Promises." *The Province*, May 24, 1975, p. 5.

Sutton, S.B., ed. *Civilizing American Cities: A Selection of Frederick Law Olmsted's Writings on City Landscapes.* Massachusetts Institute of Technology, 1971.

Taylor, Tom. *Glimpses: World War II, West Vancouver. Through the Eyes of the Papers and the Paper Boy.* Vancouver: Vancouver Desktop Publishing Centre, ca. 2004.

Todd, Douglas. "Why Most Suburban Metro Vancouver Politicians Are Mum on Foreign Ownership." *Vancouver Sun*, January 22, 2018.

_______. "How Canada's Most Expensive Municipality Grew Alert to Foreign Capital." *Vancouver Sun,* January 27, 2018.

Tomlinson, Kathy. "Out of the Shadows." *The Globe and Mail*, September 10, 2016. Updated November 12, 2017.

Twombly, Robert, ed. *Frederick Law Olmsted: Essential Texts.* New York: W.W. Norton, 2010.

Upper Lands Study Review Working Group. *Upper Lands Study Review, Final Report.* Part One: Recommendations, June 1, 2015.

Walden, Sarah Phillis. *A History of West Vancouver.* M.A. thesis, UBC, 1947.

Walker, J., Alexander and Harland Bartholomew and Associates. ["A Six Part Planning Report on West Vancouver"], 1946.

Watanabe, Kiriko, et al. *Selwyn Pullan: Photographing Mid-Century West Coast Modernism*. Vancouver: Douglas & McIntyre, 2012.

"West Vancouver." *BC Magazine.* April 1912.

West Vancouver Community Foundation. "Vital Signs." 2016.

West Vancouver Town Planning Commission. "Population Density." 1945.

Willoughby, P.A. "A Brief on the 'British Properties' Development, West Vancouver, B.C." 1959. West Vancouver Archives.

Wilmot, Jennifer, compiler. "Diversifying History: Oral Histories from North Vancouver's Iranian Community." Prepared for the North Vancouver Archives.

Memorial Park, 2017. *Photo by John Moir*

Simons house, 1969. Erickson and Massey architects; Bruno Freschi, project designer.
Photo by Selwyn Pullan

ENDNOTES

INTRODUCTION

1 Richard Florida, *Who's Your City,* p. 164.
2 *The Economist,* July 22–28, 2017, p. 64.
3 Ebenezer Howard, *Garden Cities*, p. 34.

CHAPTER 1

4 Jane Jacobs, *American Cities,* p. 310.
5 The *Vancouver Province*, June 30, 1926.
6 Major Matthews, *Early Vancouver,* Vol. II, p. 72.
7 *Vancouver Sun*, November 5, 1931.
8 Francis Caulfeild fonds, West Vancouver Archives.
9 *Ted Baynes, "The Dramatic Replanning of West Vancouver in 1944."*
10 *Former councillor Ted Baynes interviewed by Peter Hall, February 25, 1988.*
11 *Baynes interviewed by Peter Hall, February 25, 1988.*
12 *Former councillor Ted Baynes to Reeve Leyland, June 14, 1940.*
13 *Vancouver Sun,* May 27, 1969.
14 Rod Day, "Citizens' Planning Forum," unpublished article.
15 Rod Day.
16 Mike Steele, *North and West Voice*, January 1997.
17 *North Shore News*, March 6, 1988, p. 3.
18 *North Shore News*, February 14, 1988, p. 6.
19 Donald Barcham, "The Large House Syndrome," May 1988.
20 Donald Barcham.
21 Florida, *The New Urban Crisis*, p. 159.

CHAPTER 2

22 *News Advertiser*, March 12, 1890.
23 *West Vancouver News*, November 24, 1938.
24 "A View of Horseshoe Bay," ca. 1948. West Vancouver Memorial Library clipping file, "Horseshoe Bay."
25 Mrs. Greenwood interview.
26 Mrs. Greenwood interviewed by Rupert Harrison.
27 Tom Taylor, *Glimpses: World War II, West Vancouver. Through the Eyes of the Papers and the Paper Boy*, p. 246.
28 Lance Berelowitz, *Dream City*, p. 223.
29 Florida, *Who's Your City*, p. 184.
30 Florida, p. 166.
31 Heinz Berger, *An Adventure on Two Continents,* p. 54.
32 Berger, p. 81.

33 Alan Jessup, quoted by Jim McDowell in the *Vancouver Sun,* October 27, 1979.
34 *Vancouver Sun*, October 27, 1979.
35 Berger, 155.

CHAPTER 3

36 Discussion of the life of the Squamish people after settlers began to arrive relies largely on Brendan O'Donnell, "Indian and non-Native Use of the Capilano River: An Historical Perspective," Fisheries and Oceans, Canada, Policy and Program Planning, Native Affairs Division Issue 5, n.d.
37 Reverend George Forbes papers, UBC Special Collections.
38 Kevin Griffin, "Canada 150: Joe Capilano Rose to Prominence with 1906 Visit to King Edward in London," *Vancouver Sun,* May 10, 2017.
39 Eric Jamieson, *The Native Voice*, p. 39.
40 O'Donnell, 26.
41 O'Donnell, 28.
42 "West Vancouver Town Planning Commission Report," (1945), p. 6.
43 Simon Baker, with Verna Kirkness, *Khot-la-Cha, The Autobiography of Simon Baker*, p. 100.
44 A Development Plan for the Squamish," Acres Western Limited (1968), p. 56.
45 *North Shore News*, October 20, 1995, p. 4.
46 *North Shore News*, February 28, 1990.
47 *North Shore News*, September 2, 1992.

CHAPTER 4

48 Frederic Mulally, *The Silver Salver: The Story of the Guinness Family,* p. 3.
49 *Vancouver Sun*, August 22, 1936.
50 Don Luxton, *Lions Gate Bridge*, pp. 142–43.
51 See *Lions Gate Bridge*, by Don Luxton and Lilia D'Acres for a full description of the building of Lions Gate Bridge, including Taylor's role.
52 *The Globe and Mail*, June 18, 1994, p. A6.
53 The *Province,* April 25, 1951.
54 "Memories of a Man." *Lions Gate Times,* October 7, 1965, p. 2.
55 *Tally Ho*, March 11, 1955.
56 Rod Day, "Citizens' Planning Forum."
57 *Tally Ho,* March 15, 1960.
58 Rod Day, "Citizens' Planning Forum."
59 *Rodgers Creek Neighbourhood Plan*, p. 12.
60 Sartori Environmental Services, "Rodgers Creek Area 6—Phase 2 Development Permit Environmental Management Plan," North Vancouver, August 2007.

61 *Rodgers Creek: A History and Summary of the Area Development Plan.*
62 *Envisioning Notebook*, 2000, p. 25.
63 Cypress Village report, p. 14.

CHAPTER 5

64 Harold Kalman, *A History of Canadian Architecture*, Vol. 2, p. 834.
65 The *Province*, October 1, 1975, p. 6. Rpt. from the *Province*, September 1, 1950.
66 Francis Lovegrove, *West Vancouver News,* September 7, 1950.
67 "The Surging Community: West Vancouver" (promotional pamphlet).
68 Derrick Humphreys, *The Making of a Grey Panther*, p. 258.

CHAPTER 6

69 Jonathan Chancey, *The Story of Architecture*, p. 185.
70 Roy Jessimam, quoted in Greg Bellerby, *The West Coast Modern House: Vancouver Residential Architecture*, p. 12.
71 *Western Homes and Living,* October 1950, p. 15.
72 Barry Downs, *Melding Architecture with Landscape*, p. 9.
73 Downs, p. 24.
74 Kalman, pp. 794–795.
75 Bellerby, *The West Coast Modern House*, p. 158.
76 [Sylvia Lauder], Introduction to *Lauder Bros., Custom Home Builders 1948–1997*, 2002.

CHAPTER 7

77 Maisie Hurley, quoted in Jamieson, 259.

CHAPTER 8

78 Yes, that's what the census says, but the volatility of the international real estate market and the under-reporting by many owners of Canadian income probably means that the actual median income is much higher.
79 The *Province*, July 19, 2016.
80 *Vancouver Sun*, March 24, 2016.
81 *The Globe and Mail*, September 10, 2016, updated November 12, 2017.

Downs house, 1979. *Photo by Barry Downs*

INDEX